From Mumbai to Mecca

First published in Great Britain in 2007 by
Haus Publishing Ltd,
70 Cadogan Place
London SW1X 9AH
www.hauspublishing.co.uk

This first paperback edition published in 2017

Originally published under the title *Zu den heiligen Quellen des Islam.
Als Pilger nach Mekka und Medina* by Ilija Trojanow
© 2004 Piper Verlag GmbH, München
Translation copyright © 2007, 2017 Rebecca Morrison

The moral rights of the author have been asserted

A CIP catalogue record for this book is available from the
British Library

ISBN: 978-1-909961-51-7

Typeset in Garamond by MacGuru Ltd

Printed and bound in the UK

From Mumbai to Mecca

A Pilgrimage to the Holy Sites of Islam

by
Ilija Trojanow

Translated by Rebecca Morrison

 ArmchairTraveller

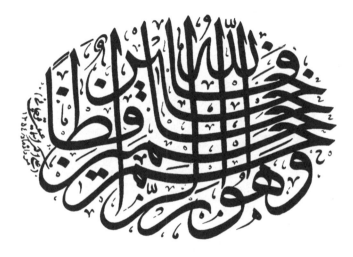

To all the brothers and sisters who were by my side to help before, during and after the Hajj.

Prologue

⟨∂⟩⟨∂⟩⟨∂⟩⟨∂⟩⟨∂⟩⟨∂⟩⟨∂⟩⟨∂⟩

Ancient both as a form as well as a tradition, literary travel writing about the Hajj – *Rihla* in Arabic, *Safarnameh* in Persian – has been in existence for over one thousand years. These are accounts of the Muslim pilgrimage as the culmination of all desires, the unique time-out that is as rich in trial and tribulation as it is in rewards and delight. Whether the words are those of Naser-e Khusrau, Ibn Jubayr, Ibn Battuta, Mohammed Farahani, Hossein Kazemzadeh or Mohammed Asad, to name some of the most renowned names in this tradition – they all aimed to be honest, informative and enlightening without glossing over their experience or concealing their suffering, nor were they sparing in their criticism of the conditions they saw and the way Islam was being lived and practised. There has always existed a deep chasm between the promise and the reality of the Hajj, which lends a particular tension to the accounts. It is, therefore, to this author, a matter of importance as well as honour to be following this tradition.

A common feature for all Muslim narrators who write about their Hajj experience is that they do not place their own feelings in the foreground and only on occasion delve into their own sensitivities. The travel writer who allows the world to revolve around his own person and psyche is a more recent Western phenomenon. Among the half dozen or so non-Muslim Hajj authors – as varied in character as in their alibis or masquerades; slaves, short-lived converts, researchers and adventurers – two accounts stand out: those of Johann Ludwig Burckhardt of Switzerland, and the British explorer Sir Richard Francis Burton. Characterised by their painstaking effort for precision, both accounts are predominantly free of ideological slander or racist perniciousness. It is indicative that both authors, who couldn't be categorized as practicing Muslims, are regarded at least as sympathisers of an ideal Islam.

Allah is the Arabic word for God that is used by Arab Muslims, as well as Arabic-speaking Christians and Jews alike – much in the same way the French refer to God as *Dieu*. However, the use of the word Allah in an English context only serves to further alienate and differentiate the Islamic concept of God, as though it fundamentally differs from what is familiar to Christians. This misconception culminates in the nonsensical but all-too-common translation of the creed of faith as: And there is no God but Allah. Since there is no other God than God, since He is without name, because intangible, I will use the term Allah only when quoting.

Departure

A long queue of people stretched from the first check-in point, all identically dressed. The queue snaked through the terminal as far as the exit and beyond. A few paces away, a glass wall separated those waiting to depart from their relatives who were dressed in a burst of every-day colours. Gathering for the final farewell, they were excited, boisterous, and packed in tightly, on the look-out for one last wave or some other parting gesture of assurance. Although it was the middle of the night, it was warm and humid outside, but inside the chilly breath of the air-conditioning was seeping through and those waiting were cold in their light attire. The men were clad in two pieces of white cloth; one wrapped around their hips, the other draped over their shoulders, while the women were somewhat better protected in their full-length white robes and headscarves. Outside, there was a bazaar-like atmosphere – luggage surrounded by extended families, the thoroughfare blocked by people and sacks of rice – an air of vibrant celebration reigned, tempered by a creeping sense of uncertainty. Inside, the festive atmosphere was muted: We stood in a single, orderly line and inched our baggage trolleys forward, calmly, as though knowing what was in store for us.

Picking me up from home a few hours before, they had been emotional, even more excited than relatives or friends are on an occasion such as this. After all, they were the ones who had prepared me for the journey throughout the preceding months, had answered my questions and shared in my growing anticipation – they had borne witness to my transformation into a pilgrim. They bought me the *ihram* I was to wear, those two white wraps of light terry cloth, and now they helped me put them on. As they gathered round for the obligatory photo, they suppressed their smiles like restive children.

After a brief, solitary prayer, I stood in the middle of the room, feeling vulnerable and at the mercy of my friends. They looked me up and down, expressed their satisfaction, yet their approval made me suddenly aware of the new distance between us. By donning the ihram, I had adopted the pilgrim state and as such, we were no longer equal. Not only because I was blessed in a wonderful way, but also now in many respects, I would have to conform to almost a reversal of the rules they followed as believers who are not embarking on the Hajj. In ihram I was forbidden to cut my hair or nails, wear tailored clothing, head coverings, substantial shoes, or socks, or to use aftershave. I was also not allowed to cover my face, have sexual intercourse, kill animals (with the exception of certain dangerous or poisonous ones), or engage in any fight or quarrel. After performing the pilgrimage, I would return to my friends and resume the familiar norms, distinct however as a Hajji – someone worthy of respect for having performed the pilgrimage to Mecca.

'Can you recite the *Labbeik**?' one of my friends asked, and I uttered the first line, a little diffidently at first, but with increasing confidence as the others joined in, and we recited, on the 16th floor of a Mumbai skyscraper, the call of the pilgrim in unison:

Labbeik, Allahumma, Labbeik;
Labbeik, La Sharika Laka, Labbeik;
Innal hamda Wal Nimata Laka Wal Mulk;
Laa Sharika Lak

[Here I am, O' God, at Thy Command! Here I am at
  Thy command!
Thou art without other; Here I am at Thy Command!
Praise, blessings and dominion are Thine! Thou art
  without associate.]

On the way to the airport, I collected the various requests for specific prayers from my brothers. Prayers spoken on behalf of someone else are more effective than prayers spoken on one's own behalf. Intercession is a very powerful concept in Islam, and it is believed that when in Mecca 'the gates of heaven are open' to one's prayers. Most powerful of all, however, are the prayers undertaken for a fellow Muslim beside the Kaaba in Mecca, and at the tomb of Prophet Muhammad (pbuh) in Medina. I promised to pray for mothers, for wives in the final stages of pregnancy, for newlyweds, and for the recently deceased.

---

* definition in the glossary at the end of the book

We took our leave of one another at Terminal 2, known at this time of year as the 'Hajj Terminal'. Burhan, who had been particularly helpful in the lead-up, took me to one side conspiratorially and said:

'You will experience things, which will seem strange to you. Hajjis can behave like madmen. You will perhaps question the sense of some rituals: the running back and forth between hills, or the stoning of the pillars. And you will be taken aback by the behaviour of many Hajjis, but you have to understand – it all stems from love. A lover is not always rational in his actions, or how he expresses his emotions and aims to please his beloved. He is excessive and unrestrained.' So saying, Burhan embraced me warmly, and I joined the line of people.

It was the colour green I noticed first, then the writing: Cosmic Travel. The man in front of me with a small son – his wealth apparent in an ihram of fine cloth and an elegant pair of spectacles – was pushing a trolley with green luggage. A family sitting a little way off on the floor was hemmed in by Cosmic Travel bags. I looked around and there were a number of people carrying two green travel bags as I was, one large and one small, with the tour company's logo on them. We belonged to the same group, all of us dependent on our tour guides who enjoyed the privilege of performing the Hajj every year. The guide I knew best was Hamidbhai, a chain-smoker with great bags under his eyes and a protruding lower lip that lent him a constantly sleepy air even in the midst of hectic activity. He could certainly smile; indeed his eyes sparkled with a general amusement at the world and people, but it was one that was only very occasionally expressed in a joke. He wasn't the sort of man you would warm to immediately, but after spending any time with him, it was impossible not to like him.

Hamidbhai was up at the check-in counter, overseeing the checking-in of our luggage. The pilgrims may have been lightly attired but they definitely weren't travelling light. Trading has always been part of the Hajj since the pre-Islamic (*Jahiliyya*) period. Bedouins poured into Mecca not only to visit the shrines of gods, but also to trade at the Great Market, and the Prophet (pbuh) – more considerate of human needs than founders of other religions – permitted an activity that provided both motivation for, and financing of, the journey. Sacks of basmati rice were piled high by the Air India counter; trolleys so laden they could scarcely be pushed, and so numerous that the non-trading pilgrims found themselves clambering over boxes and sacks to reach the check-in counter. In an age where entire time zones can be crossed in a matter of hours, the way to Mecca was still paved with obstacles.

Hamidbhai handed me one of the better boarding cards. While Hajj flights have no official division of classes, places on the upper deck of a Boeing 747 are simply more comfortable. I was glad at the prospect of a restful first night on a journey where sleeplessness was a given. One of the employees from the travel agency who had sincerely shared in my delight when my visa came through, made an impassioned plea: Would I pray that he, too, be granted to perform the Hajj the following year? I readily agreed, knowing that there would be plentiful opportunities to fulfil all these pledges. The other passengers in Terminal 2

– business travellers on their way to Singapore, yoga tourists returning to Paris – all gaped in amazement at the sight of men in archaic clothing on mobile phones placing their final calls in the winding queue for passport control.

∽∾∽∾∽

Every journey begins before one sets off on it; preparation for the Hajj, for the pilgrimage to Mecca, is a believer's vocation and the reward for his life's work. From childhood, when he first learns that the Hajj is a duty required of every Muslim, he yearns for it. And if he does not feel the compulsion from within, his nearest and dearest give him a firm helping hand, urging him as they would any Muslim who can financially afford to perform the Hajj, until he yields to the inevitable. Facing the *qibla*, the direction of each of his prayers reminds him daily of the presence of Mecca. Once a year he witnesses the excitement and effort as relatives depart, seen off in pomp and circumstance at the airport, and in some places at the railway station or the main market place.

In the weeks leading up to the official days of the pilgrimage, the *imam* elaborates on the significance of the Hajj and the duties of the pilgrims in his *khutbah*, the sermon preceding the Friday prayers. The holy law decrees, he explains, that one's familial and business affairs be sorted out before departure. The pilgrim must leave sufficient money for his family and have no outstanding debts. If his neighbour is in need, one *hadith* states, the trip must be postponed. For the Hajj is not only an individual pilgrimage, it is a communal

8

congregation, an entreaty of the *Ummah*. Most important of all, is that the prospective pilgrim divests himself of burdens and failings in advance: *Provide well for yourselves: the best provision is piety.* (2:197). While the Hajj will purge him of all sins, it will not make a better person of him. He who embarks on it a liar or hypocrite, will return a liar or hypocrite. The Hajj is not an end in itself, it is not effective on its own – a poorly executed Hajj is of less worth than no Hajj at all. Since the Hajj is not only a pinnacle of one's life but also a considerable financial undertaking, the believer has to save up for a long time, for decades sometimes, and the year prior to his departure brings a plethora of special prayers and rituals to learn.

Arrival

Only once you are there, do you see the Holy City.

In the first of many waiting rooms at Jeddah Airport, we were welcomed in the languages of the Ummah: Hos geldiniz, mabuhay, selamat dotang, hu soo dhawanda, bemvindo, bienvenue, karibuni, sanon dezuwa. The last members of a Turkish group were vacating the room, and behind us were Central Asian pilgrims speaking Russian and a language I didn't recognise. In the first room we filled out the forms for entering the country, which were checked by several officials passing through the rows; then we were led through to the next room and took a seat on the benches, with women on the left and men on the right. An hour later, our entry papers were inspected by a uniformed man up at the counter and computer-legible magnetic strips were stuck to our passports, after which we were guided through to the third hall where our baggage was thoroughly searched by customs officials in the reclaim area. Our group's luggage was heaved and stacked onto trolleys by dark-skinned workers and pushed out. The final step in the procedure took place at a square kiosk, open on all four sides, outside the terminal: the financial formalities. We handed over cheques to the value of around £250, in exchange for a double-sided insert for our passports that contained various vouchers to be redeemed against bus travel to Mecca, onwards to Medina, and from Medina back to Jeddah.

We were outside at last. The smell of leather, diesel and cleaning detergent intermingled with the slight night breeze that rustled around us. Between ourselves and the sky, a solid light beige roof emulated vast tents, a multitude of domes elegantly suspended over an area of several square kilometres, all part of allegedly the largest airport complex in the world. The pilgrims were huddled in groups, some already clad in ihram, others still in their local clothes. Often they entered following a flag-bearer, like athletes entering an Olympic stadium – some groups in formation, others in confused disarray. Their place of origin was detailed on their lapels or their backs, information about their region, town and travel group listed under another small flag, to prevent them from going astray, presumably. The tented hall was divided into areas according to nationality, though not in any obvious order, and not strictly adhered to either – we Indians found a berth in the Pakistan sector.

We waited there for seven hours, not knowing what we were waiting for, and slurped tea with condensed milk out of plastic cups – the first of many to come. There were gaps in the roof, between the tents, through which beams of sunlight slanted in – harsh light that criss-crossed the floor in a series of canals. Once, Hamidbhai told us, crouching down during a break from his negotiations with officials, the airport procedure had dragged on for 20 hours. In days gone by, pilgrims were sometimes kept at Jeddah's harbour for days on end. The delay, once attributed to the greed of local profiteers and the Ottoman administrators, was now due to a complex bureaucratic system developed by the Saudi Arabian government to keep control of the pilgrims. At the airport all passports are collected and not returned to the pilgrims until they return to the airport weeks later – but they accompany us throughout the journey – incognito, so to speak. They are kept in a bag next to the drivers or guides, and have sometimes been known to disappear into the gaping shelves of bureaucratic offices in Mecca or Medina where relocating one could take ages – as I was to discover.

⟡⟡⟡

The road from Jeddah to Mecca must be the most-travelled road on the Arabian Peninsula. At its start, the highway was strewn with rubbish that had collected in the ditches on either side but as we moved further away from the city, the desert became cleaner. After a few kilometres the road snaked over a line of low hills to the Bahra Plain. Light-coloured sand clung to the slopes of glowering, forbidding hills as we drove towards the main range of the Western Arabian mountains. An archway over the highway, depicting the Qur'an open upon a lectern, indicated the border to Miquat, the area around Mecca where pilgrims must be dressed in the ihram. Later, after certain rituals have been performed, the ihram may then be removed. On the bus, all garbed in white, we were shivering in the blast of the air-conditioning. The road had been so sturdily built a century ago that strong mules could complete the journey in six to seven hours. Subject to waits at checkpoints, and what with the traffic jams on the last few kilometres, we were hardly much quicker.

We were unaware that we had finally reached the valley in which the holy city is cradled 200 metres above sea level. Suddenly we stopped at a crossroads surrounded by hills – wherever you stand in Mecca, hills obstruct the view. Buildings rose up in every direction, ascending the hills until their strength petered out, and grey city yielded to grey rock.

The city's real name is Makkah, but like all places of extraordinary spiritual importance, it has an impressive list of eulogistic names: 'Mother of Cities', 'The Noble One' and 'The Place of the Faithful' are among the more straightforward ones. If mentioned in speech or writing, it is considered proper to supersede it with *dhadaha allahu 'azmatan wa kerama* as a sign of respect – may God the Almighty exalt it.

The bus drew up in front of a *mu'allim*'s office, also called a *mutawwif*, or local guide – a figure essential to every group. As we waited in the bus, a young man got in and without saying a word distributed drinks and snacks as part of the organised care programme we would experience at every stage of the pilgrimage whenever we took a break, stopped, or arrived anywhere. This was to be the first constant, the second – the screaming Saudi Arabian – we would witness when our bus driver took a wrong turn, misinformed perhaps by our travel guide. Stuck in a tunnel where pilgrims were being dropped off, the bus driver vented his anger in a hysterical outburst, a high-octane tirade of swear words. There was no diminuendo as he manoeuvred the bus out of the underpass, nor did he calm down when he had turned, yelping like a tyke until we arrived at last. It was with some relief when we got out, and one look was enough to appease us: There, less than 200 metres from where we stood, was the Grand Mosque. Moreover, our guesthouse looked directly onto the Haram al-Sharif – which houses the Kaaba.

'We couldn't have hoped for anything better,' a pilgrim behind me said.

Shouldering our green bags, we gathered in the reception lobby and were sorted into groups – men without female companions slept eight to a small room, four beds up against the walls with four mattresses between them like a scout camp. I lay down on the mattress closest to the bathroom, and the door, and exhaled deeply.

The First Prayer

CRCRCRCRCRCRCRCRCR

When I made my way outside, following the call to prayer, albeit rather tardily, I noticed that a very wide, steep road separated the first row of buildings – of which our guesthouse was one – from the Grand Mosque. As far as the eye could see – down the street and across to the impressive forecourt – every cubic metre was packed with pilgrims who had spread their rugs and mats in preparation for the afternoon prayer. There was hardly any place left for latecomers. And thus my first prayer was spoken between a gutter and a Sudanese street hawker who seemed to be the only person not taking the slightest notice of the ritual. It was the first of many prayers to be spoken in apparently incongruous places: in the shadow cast by police jeeps, from behind shop windows, at highway junctions, in shopping centres, in front of barber shops and next to street drains. On the Hajj you learn to pray anywhere and everywhere, and as prayer penetrates the nooks and crannies of the everyday, the stuff of banality, one's own perspective on prayer, changes as it steps beyond the mosque to become omnipresent.

Having embarked on my prayer a little late, I would need slightly longer than the others to complete it. I was just uttering the concluding *tashahhud* when the quiet unified mass around me broke into a seething tumult. There was no regard shown to my prayer, as I was used to in Mumbai. People didn't mind stepping on my prayer mat, usually regarded as an intimate space, and disturbing me; knees barged into me, feet trod on my mat, cloth brushed against my head and face. When I did stand up it was to find myself in the middle of an African street market, replete with determined hawkers with voices like lassoes – rolls of cloth, strings of prayer beads, caps and sandals were laid-out on squares of material, and throngs of pilgrims from all over the world pressed in.

Indians and Pakistanis in *kurta pyjamas*, the Anatolian fez, Afghans in *sharwanis* and heavy waistcoats, embroidered black caps from Tashkent, Arabs from the Gulf region in the long white *jellabah*, the red- and white-checked head-covering of the Bedouins, Swahilis in *kanzus*, *topis* both of the soft and stiff variety, Central Asian women in matronly dresses, the *hijab* their only concession to the place and occasion, Iranian holy men in billowing robes, white and coloured topis, mysterious figures in *burq'o*, simple and elaborate head coverings, Moroccans in richly embroidered jellabahs at the hem, the laboured turbans of the ayatollahs, West Africans in vivid colours and loose *boubous*, caps perched like crests, Turks in heavy greenish-grey uniforms and fellahin in *kaftan* and *gubba*. Even within the scarves there existed a wide range and variety, plain and festive, wrapped around heads or drawn-up over them. The diversity was without comparison; it refuted the claim that Islam had washed away all cultural differences in the countries where it had taken root. While united by a mutual ritual of prayer (bar the odd difference in the position of a hand or finishing of a movement in the four traditional Islamic schools), anyone not in ihram, having performed the first sequence of rites, was wearing traditional dress. Never before have I seen so few trousers or shirts in such a crowd of people.

It was evident that traditional, local dress was still worn in Islamic cultural circles, not in a folkloric manner, but rather on a daily basis. In Christian societies however, a uniform European fashion has taken over, as in the Philippines, for example. The western dress of the Filipinos would have looked awfully dull next to the elegant Indonesians in their exuberant, bright batik shirts with their abstract patterns, or floral prints and birds, worn over their sarong. Their jackets a festive colour, reflected in the headscarves, and echoed in other scarves worn by the women.

Rituals

There's not a pilgrim who can forget his
first glimpse of the Kaaba.

It was less than a two-minute walk from our hotel to one of the 99 entrances to the Haram; the holiest of refuges. If it hadn't been for the teeming crowds, that is. Instead, it took us quarter of an hour – of jostling and being brushed against by the throng – until we were eventually allowed through to reach the interior of the Grand Mosque. Hamidbhai, whom I'd met on the pavement after prayers, had offered to guide me through the first of the obligatory rituals. Two other Indian pilgrims joined us, and together we cut a path through the dense crowds. A hand on the shoulder of the man in front was our only navigational aid. Women often tied their veils together to prevent getting lost, or held hands so tightly that it was impossible to pass through. We clung to each other, too, repeating the call of the pilgrim intoned by Hamidbhai: *Labbeik, Allahumma, Labbeik; Labbeik, La Sharika Laka, Labbeik,* until we were chanting the staccato-like eulogy in harmony.

By the entrance, Hamidbhai drew me to him and spoke earnestly:

'The wish you express when you first lay eyes on the Kaaba will come true. For now keep your eyes downcast. Don't look up until I tell you.'

I left my sandals at the entrance where thousands of other pairs were piled, and stepped barefoot through the Abdul-Aziz Gate, my eyes fixed on the marble floor. Pummelled by the crowd, reciting the *talbiyah* to myself, nervous as a schoolboy, I edged my way forward, retreating deeper and deeper into prayer. The chorus all around me was a symphony of individual voices and others in perfect unison.

In front of the mosque we'd had to elbow a little, and push a bit so as not to be shoved out the way – inside was a veritable struggle. Apparently hardly any pilgrims were heeding the pleas of the guides to tread carefully, not to push, nor to behave coarsely, rudely, or egotistically, in short: not to sin. The sheer mass of people forced one to determinedly hold one's own and disrespect spread like a rash. Part of me was consumed by aggressive panic, another part was afloat.

'Pray,' Hamidbhai said as we descended the steps, 'pray that you will always only pray for the right things. Pray for the appropriateness of your prayers.'

And then, a few *Labbeik* cycles later, he said: 'Look up now.'

It was a moving sight. Immediate. Free of analysis or reflection. The simple form of the Kaaba, the black brocade – the *kiswah*, as beautiful as a bridal veil – the inner court awash with pilgrims swarming around the immovable cube.

The atmosphere was one of excitement and happiness, crackling with the dreams of a lifetime being fulfilled at that moment. And without thinking, without having prepared myself for it, a sharp, powerful wish welled up in me, and my eyes filled with tears. We carefully ploughed our way through the multitudes who were sitting at the edge of the inner court, blocking the way to the Kaaba, and abandoned ourselves to the *tawaf*, the ritualistic circumambulation of the Kaaba seven times.

We were almost submerged by the masses, but the Kaaba, which we were not meant to look at during the tawaf, became a reliable focal point nonetheless, its corners pointing to the four directions of the sky. In days gone by they had been named after the great caravan routes: Yemen, Syria, Iraq and Egypt. The small golden door in the grey cube was locked (once a year it is opened for the ceremonial cleansing in rosewater, a ritual undertaken in the presence of the Saudi king), and the surface remained unadorned apart from the black kiswah cloth, its ends folded back to signify Hajj-time, but perhaps also to protect it from the eager fingers of many pilgrims.

On the outskirts of the overflowing crowd, it was unthinkable to perform the first three circles at a gentle run as prescribed, 'chest thrust out like a brave soldier', right shoulder bared. The tawaf begins at the Black Stone, a mysterious relic from ancient times – a meteorite perhaps, according to legend once white as limestone, but turned black over time by all the sinful lips and hands that have touched it. A line the width of a foot leads eastwards from the Black Stone, marking the beginning and end of the tawaf; each time we completed a circle, we paused, and with the palms of our hands held high called *Bismillah Allahu Akbar,* then, to receive the blessing emanating from the stone, held our hands to our lips.

The people's excitement interrupted the flow of my prayers; there was pushing and shoving, someone clutched my shoulder, someone else almost tore the cloth from my upper body, and collectively we fought for air. Nearby men were gesticulating desperately: a woman had fainted and was lying on the ground, she was surrounded by pilgrims trying to attract the attention of some medical staff.

We had just laboriously completed two circles when the call to night prayer came. A miracle took place: The wild throng of hectic circling stopped and suddenly everyone found their place and position in respect to the brothers and sisters around them; a stillness crystallised, and out of it rose a well-tuned voice that opened the prayers.

If the whole world could be gazed upon at the time of prayer, the sight would be reminiscent of these concentric circles of praying people facing the Kaaba. At prayers the Ummah itself becomes an Islamic ornament, and we were standing and kneeling a mere dozen steps from the centre of this living pattern.

After prayers we stood up immediately, rather than remaining in personal prayer as is customary, which would have proven dangerous in this tempestuous atmosphere. Soon the number of pilgrims had notably thinned and the tawaf continued without further incident. We squeezed past palanquins on which the frail were transported round the Kaaba at a trot. I bumped into a pilgrim reading prayers from a sheet of paper – some groups were following a prayer leader, whose one-line chants they repeated in unison. I was overtaken by an Arab partaking in a lively conversation on his mobile phone, interrupting his chat only to utter '*Bismillah Allahu Akbar*'. An old man from Northern Pakistan embraced me, and together we completed the final circuit, exhilarated, our prayers and our steps in tandem, and for a short while he was both a grandfather and a brother to me.

After the tawaf you are supposed to recite a short prayer at the Maqam Ibrahim – the place where Ibrahim (the Biblical Abraham) once stood – the impressions of ancient footsteps clearly visible on the stone. In those crowds it would have been thoughtless, not to mention utterly impractical, to lie prostrate there, and certainly not conducive to prayer. Instead, we prayed a little way off beside two men who were racked with sobs, each overwhelmed by the place and the magnitude of the moment. Away from the frenzied warmth of the crowd, they appeared fragile, tender and uncertain.

We didn't make it to the well of Zamzam, underground nowadays, as the crowd bore us away. But in the mosque there was a collection of tan-coloured containers filled with water and two rows of plastic cups – clean ones to the left; to the right, the used. It was tasty water, rich in minerals, which is perhaps why it had been described by many an earlier pilgrim as brackish and foul – you are to meant to drink as much of it as you can. My '*ulama* brothers had expressed only one wish: that I bring them back some holy water, their favoured fluid for breaking their Ramadan fasting. Zamzam water used to be terribly expensive; today it is free – only the container comes at a cost.

The subsequent *sa'ee* (the running), the seven *shawt*, or traversing of the distance, between the hills of Safa and Marwah, had sounded like a endurance test in a parched valley, almost like a kind of self-chastisement and penance of some sacrifice when it was first described to me. In reality, we simply crossed through a side chamber of the mosque and entered a corridor about 200 metres long – it may have sloped a bit and got steeper further along, but in general it was rather like the corridors you might find connecting two halls of a trade fair or in a Las Vegas hotel. Neon strip lights cast a harsh sterile glow over the splendour and colour of the marble – there were even some elaborate chandeliers for beautification. The 'summits' of the hills had been left in their natural state. We could feel the black rock beneath our feet as we turned to the Kaaba and spoke the assigned prayer before we set off along the polished walkway. The two narrow lanes in the middle of the corridor were intended for wheelchair users, but were used instead by the swifter of foot. As I walked at a moderate pace with my Indian brothers, from the corner of my eye I saw elegant African figures gliding by in long proud strides, their arms swinging like scythes, and I thought I could read a certain disapproval in their faces for those performing the sa'ee with less physical vigour.

The legend which forms the basis of this rite goes way back to the ancient story of the family that all three of the monotheistic religions regard as their forefathers:

the family of Ibrahim. The mother of his first son Ismail (Ishmael), the spurned Hagar, was abandoned in the desert with her infant son, armed only with the power of prayer. She climbed the hill of Safa to look for water, then ran to the hill of Marwah, back and forth, driven more by desperation than reason. She was close to giving up, when she noticed her child strike his foot against the earth in play, and at that very place the water started to flow.

There, where Hagar had once crossed a stony, drained riverbed, every Hajji was now to pick up pace in remembrance of her tribulation – the 30-metre-long stretch is marked by two green neon lights. Women are not required to run, but a group of Nigerian women ignored such unnecessary regard to their gender, and raced, whooping, from one boundary of light to the other.

Just a generation back, Hamidbhai told me, the sa'ee had not been roofed, and shops had lined the path. His parents had walked through sand and had bought presents on the way. In general, the Hajj had become much more comfortable as those who had completed theirs 10 or 20 years earlier confirmed. Almost too easy, in fact, for surely some toil was required to cleanse yourself of sins? He who seeks greatness must endure great sacrifice, Ibn Jubayr wrote in the 12th century.

Since it is permissible to insert breaks into the sa'ee – hours or even several days – we rested after completing three sections, perching on the steps of a row of barbers next to one of the side entrances. A barber stood in every doorway, dramatically wielding a razor blade and noisily courting the favour of those who had just completed their rituals.

The shaving of the head is the final duty, but there were few distinguishing features between the booths and, as is often the case at a bazaar, choices by those new to the place were determined by the persistence or charm of the individual barbers. Hamidbhai warned us about botchers who in their haste (a million heads to be shorn) often bloodied scalps, and recommended instead that we use a barber near our hotel, a compatriot of course, who had gained a fine reputation over time as one who did not spill blood. I could have chosen an easier alternative – the cutting of a mere lock of hair, as is requisite for women – but such omissions mean a decrease in blessings and respect.

Our *Umrah*, a mini-Hajj, was concluded an hour later with a cleanly shaved head (the barber praised me for choosing the blade over the electric razor), many a lengthy exchange of well-wishes and embraces, and a midnight snack in Hamidbhai's room. He presented me with a new pair of sandals, as he felt responsible for the disappearance of the footwear that I had left at the Abdul-Aziz Gate. With the Umrah we had fulfilled the rituals which visitors to Mecca perform whatever the season; we could remove our ihram, and were now ready for the main part of the Hajj, that strict appointment with God and the community of believers.

Preparation

The preparation for my Hajj had begun in a small room off Crawford Market, a densely populated, lively, predominantly Muslim quarter of Mumbai. It was December and the travelling hawkers on the street that leads to the Friday Mosque were plying their wares – plastic Christmas trees from China. At the entrance to the building I'd been looking for was a *chaiwallah*, a seller of tea, whom I was to get to know well in the course of the next 12 months. He would bring tea up to us on the first floor in a wire holder, the tea in slender glasses and tin beakers of water, and wait for us to finish, which we did sitting down, in three gulps, first the water, then the tea. He boiled the tea with milk, sugar and spices in a large pot by the front door, and was there at all hours, a surly fellow who took his time to acknowledge me. The stairs creaked with age, the building, as is often the case in Mumbai, a ruin beyond the inhabited flats and offices. There was a doctor's practice on the first floor, and next to it the office of the Markazul Maarif Organisation, an NGO that aims to educate Muslims. I knocked on the door, and it was opened by a young man dressed simply in a white kurta pyjama, as all the young men would be with whom I'd spend the coming year, as well as sporting unruly beards.

He bade me welcome and showed me inside. The office was set up as a large open space with six computer terminals along the left side of the wall. On the opposite side was a long bookcase that was spilling over, and a separate cubicle at the far end, small but air-conditioned, which was the manager's office. I had come with a recommendation from a Muslim journalist and activist who was both well-known and treated with suspicion for his liberal thinking, and was thus initially given a cool, distant reception. I spoke of my interest in Islam, and the young leader told me about his organisation. It was dedicated to social work and had orphanages and hospitals in the north-east of the country. In Mumbai their main duty was to supervise 10 young 'ulama, scholars, who were experts on all religious questions, but in addition were to become competent in English and computer technology. They had been studying intensely for two years, spoke fluent English and had mastered word processing, as well as utilising the Internet. The organisation hoped that these young men would one day be in a position to write fluent, insightful articles in English to counteract the sparse, or false, information about Islam prevalent amongst members of the Indian public.

'We have to take them a step further,' the manager said.

It took just a single meeting to decide: I would teach the young men writing skills and in return would gain a more profound understanding of Islam. It was a good deal, in the spirit of the Prophet (pbuh): practical, sensible and honourable.

'You have to understand,' Burhan, the office manager, said, 'our interest in you is in how you can be of help to us. Let's make an agreement – and what comes of it will depend on both sides.'

Then he asked to see my passport and my residency permit to make photocopies.

'As an Islamic organisation,' he explained, 'we have to cover ourselves. We are under observation by the Indian secret service and they can question us at any time. We have to be ready to give them satisfactory answers. There is a lot of fear and distrust these days, and we have to tread cautiously.'

And so it was that we came together, 10 young men, who all went by the name of Qasmi, and myself, referred to as 'Sir' or 'Respected Teacher' for several months, until we were close enough that I could persuade them to call me 'Ilias' sometimes. We met three times a week. One of the men, an authority on the law, a *mufti*, became my personal teacher (although the others were always on hand to act as his assistants). After an hour, we swapped roles and I taught them in a narrow classroom with a low ceiling, which served as the library and common room.

The Kaaba

Many buildings are overwhelming to the eye, yet some, very few, overwhelm the mind. The Haram al-Sharif, the Grand Mosque at Mecca, with its numerous entrances and pillars, curves and alignments, corners and niches, all 130,000 square metres of it, is not only unfathomably large, but the ever-changing perspectives revealed to the pilgrim upon each visit also proclaim the immeasurability of God. The architecture is difficult to judge in and of itself, so closely do the pilgrims associate with the asymmetrical construction. The choreography of the rituals infuses the grey and white and green, and reaches up to the seven minarets and the seven domes. If architecture is substance filled with life, then the Haram is surely one of mankind's most beautiful buildings.

The passageways, the arches, the domes, and the galleries are indeed imposing, but without the Kaaba, impressive despite the simplicity of its architecture, they would be without effect. The golden embroidery on the black material seems almost too ornamental, a distraction from the purity of the simple, cubically conceived idea. The symbol is constantly affirmed by the pilgrims who night and day circle this sun like planets, each of their steps charging the right-angled structure with human power. It is through this interaction that *Bayt Allah*, the House of God, and the Ummah, the community of believers, emerges. It is like the holy text: it requires the devotion and the morality of the reader to come to life. The revelation is poured into a human vessel, language, and is thus dependant on the power and the effect each one creates from it and lends it.

Because of the prescribed alignment towards the Kaaba, the Haram al-Sharif is the only mosque in the world that is round. Added to, and several times in its history rebuilt from scratch after being destroyed, it was massively and expensively expanded in the 1960s. It stands, however, on the same site where it has stood on for thousands of years.

Yet however new the building materials of modern Mecca are, the place itself is old enough to owe its existence to the Zamzam source, a vein of life in the merciless desert. The Kaaba was erected in accordance with the instructions of Ibrahim, according to the Qur'an. The sacred building from its very beginnings constituted a holy site – a pertinent one for the pre-Islamic pilgrimage. In the Kaaba a plethora of idols, projections of different cults, were housed, the most popular being Allat, Uzza and Manat. This pantheon was shaped by a pragmatic liberality: among the holy figures were both Venus and the Virgin Mary, testimony to a lively religious convergence. A trading metropolis formed around this site of pilgrimage – even during the days of the Prophet (pbuh) there was a vital urbanism. While the customs and code of behaviour were still influenced by the nomads, the way of life was urban, and the buildings made of solid clay. Mecca was rich, but its wealth was very unevenly distributed; Mecca was tolerant towards gods, but harsh towards women and orphans who had no rights.

Perhaps the transition from nomad to urban culture was as overhasty as the transition from Bedouin tents to concrete palaces which the Saudi Arabians rushed into a generation ago. The result, now as then, was a broken, unjust, and violent society, and the revelation of God to His Messenger with its revolutionary concepts must have had an explosive effect at this time of crisis. The Quraysh tribe, monopolists of the source of income that was the Kaaba, feared the new religion would rob them of their privileges. After his victory over Mecca, however, the Prophet (pbuh), a leader ever open to compromise, allowed the pilgrimage to the Kaaba to continue; retaining some of its traditional rituals such as the seven circles and the running between the hills of Safa and Marwah, he ushered the pilgrimage into a new age that became the Hajj.

On the next day I walked down the steps to the Zamzam well; it was sticky and damp, and very full. On the lower left side behind glass panelling was a high-tech pumping station. Some pilgrims were standing in front of it, but they weren't interested in the pistons, they were, I discovered when I came alongside them, deep in prayer. There was an unintended comic aspect to this, as the holy Zamzam water was nowhere in sight, just a hi-tech installation of pipes, taps, containers and ventilators. Educated Muslims point out time and again that neither Zamzam water nor the

Black Stone should be worshipped – that would be poly-theism, animism – yet the scene of intense prayer to my left paid witness to a need to satisfy one's own superstitions, the expression of an inability to live out the pure doctrine, that of a monotheism free of idols.

Companions

The majority of the men I was sharing the room with were well-off independent businessmen, partners in a firm exporting women's wear, their friend, a toy importer, and an acquaintance of theirs who ran a courier service. They were all young, intent on being earnest, but not completely fulfilled by what the Hajj had to offer. Their conversations, when not centred around the complex demands of the rituals, were profane: they spoke about cricket and cars, told jokes. Two of them spent hours within the labyrinths of a game of dexterity on their Nokia phones. Like the majority of pilgrims, they were stretched by the demands imposed by having to live this religious life for several weeks. The guides demanded they spend their day in prayer and Qur'an recitation, warning them about superfluous or angry words. But the pilgrims were seized by a restlessness and often descended into chatter – it was too great a leap from hectic modern urbanite to a fakir renouncing the world. My roommates paid sincere lip service in their appreciation of *iman*, the right faith, but were content with their superficial knowledge of Islam, its legends and parables. They felt secure in their ignorance for they adhered to the laws.

During the Hajj I didn't see a single pilgrim reading a religious book. Lectures on the other hand, informative and stimulating, are part and parcel of the programme for organised groups. And the holy Qur'an, which many people open in the mosque or display on a small lectern after the common prayer is less read than recited, a sacred act in itself during which the believer reads the words out under his breath in one of seven reading styles. What is consumed in mass are the brochures with the obligatory prayers printed, particularly highly regarded for the translations they contain – and yet prayers themselves can disguise a lack of knowledge.

Abu Sufiyun, whose cigarettes I smoked when the need overcame me, became my superintendent, the one who corrected me. When his eyes were on me I felt he was measuring me up, checking whether I matched up to the religious ideals. Each of my failings or mistakes prompted a sermon. He was a law-abiding man who had never considered that laws can be expressions of meaning.

'Laws are laws,' he said. 'Liking, or understanding them has nothing to do with it.'

Perhaps his strict manner was meant to compensate for an earlier lifestyle; up until a few years ago he had been a bon vivant who enjoyed himself excessively with his friends. He was well acquainted with the glamorous, rich playground Mumbai scene and paraded this knowledge with pride. It was as though, as an expression of former mistakes, it could serve as a backdrop to display his transformation with particular clarity. Now his full beard and other characteristics in his appearance bespoke this deep belief. The patches of rough skin on the instep of his left foot were the result of fervent prayer; in the correct sitting position – disregarded by plenty of believers for comfort's sake – you put your weight on your left leg, the leg underneath, as the toes of the right foot are stretched out and slightly curled under.

'Outward attributes,' he informed me, when I voiced my doubts over their necessity, 'strengthen one's faith.'

The wild young things, the passionate mobile phone users, Nadiim, Salman and Shorab, would listen to him but seemed to favour the playing field of compromise. At the far end of the room an elderly gentleman with the blessed surname Ghalib had one of the beds, while his son, a purchase manager in a factory in Dubai, slept on the floor next to him. Mr Ghalib, a retired Air India engineer, had been a high-ranking trade union official who had attended congresses in Los Angeles and Frankfurt, and a certain attitude had stuck – a mixture of scepticism and stubbornness – that made him stand out from the others. His son, Amir, as his friends called him and I was allowed to after some lively discussions – had studied business management, and the other son was an engineer like his father. They were more highly educated than the average Indian Muslim family, and were torn by the conflict of those trying to reconcile faith and education.

His father had kept postponing the Hajj after his wife's death, Amir told me, as though discussing a silly child. He had pushed his father, persisted on the case before eventually handing his brother the task of organising the Hajj, paying for everything and presenting their father with a *fait accompli*. He had travelled from Dubai to Mumbai to ensure his father would actually get on the plane. Relations were strained between him and the family; he hadn't spoken to one of his brothers for years. The reason for this tension was two-fold: when Amir first went abroad he had earned a lot of money, 'far too much money', he said; it had been a burden for the family. He never gave the second reason but it apparently had something to do with Amir's religious change; prayers and commandments hadn't always been sacred to him – he must have been quite a loose cannon in college – the professors were frightened of him and would cross the corridor if they saw him coming. He had been a chain-smoker and had perhaps even dabbled in alcohol (it's hard to glean everything from veiled references), until one day he underwent a transformation.

On Discipline and Form

⚡⚡⚡⚡⚡⚡⚡⚡⚡⚡⚡

O f the five pillars of Islam, the Hajj is usually listed last; in first place is the declaration of faith, followed by the obligation of prayer, five times a day. The declaration of faith – *Laa ilaaha illallaahu Muhammadur rasuulullahi,* [There is only one God and Muhammad is the Prophet of God] – is as simple and straightforward as the prayer is difficult – almost incomprehensibly so.

After testing the English of my new pupils in Mumbai using a text about *al-Andalus* (it was impressively good, and their enthusiasm was great), they in turn checked my knowledge of the rudiments of the prayer and found it so threadbare that they forced out laugher to cover up the embarrassment of the situation. They were exemplary indeed in their politeness and obliging ways from the very start: the teacher must not be placed in an awkward position, even if it is one of his own making.

Even my *wazu*, the ritual washing prior to any prayer, was pathetic. My hands and feet may have been clean enough after it; however it's not the result that counts but rather the manner in which it is accomplished. We would sit in the Friday Mosque at the edge of the pool with its remarkably long red fish and dip our hand in letting our fingers glide through the water, which was cool even on the hottest day. Cleaning our fingers with careful deliberation, we would take a gulp of water, wash out our mouths, draw water up into our nose then blow it out into our left hand; then we scooped water up and raised it to our face. The face was washed three times, then the arms, also three times, from the elbow to the wrist – missing any of it meant endangering the efficacy of the prayer (once in the washroom of a shopping centre in Mecca, I forgot – hectic and distracted – to wash my right elbow, whereupon somebody poked me from behind and pointed out my mistake). After the arms, it was the head's turn. The fingers, pressed together, follow the hair down to the neck, then the balls of the thumbs stroke the sides of the head up to the forehead. Next, the ears are washed after which the *wazu* concludes with a thorough scrubbing of the feet, the dirtiest body part in this country of heat and sandals.

Hygiene is certainly one important motive for wazu, but the compulsory washing also has a spiritual objective. With every washing I became more aware of the fact that the wazu also washes away the everyday; the various stages lead to a peacefulness; the wetness refreshes and revives, and finally you embark upon prayer in a content, collected state.

The prayer itself makes the wazu seem like an easy feat. There are books devoted solely to the *salat*, and they list the numerous mistakes that can be made. Posture is important, movements equally so, the speed at which it is performed is important as, of course, is one's inner state. In the early weeks I was reprimanded for not holding my hands over my knees correctly (with fingers outstretched), and not placing them correctly on the floor (fingers pressed together and pointing forward), for not rolling my sleeves back down after washing, and not turning my arms away from my body while kneeling; for not bowing my head while standing and for looking up while sitting down. Hardly anything escaped my teachers, and after prayer I often had to stay on in the inner court afterwards. Shihabuddin, my personal teacher, was particularly observant and rigorous; he was of the opinion that you should first learn the laws of Islam before questioning their meaning. Since I tended to adopt the opposite approach, it meant that he sometimes had to be strict with me, which occasionally left me disappointed in him. He was of the conviction that discipline in faith is every bit as important as love.

One afternoon at 'asr – we had arrived late for prayer – I helplessly copied everything that Shihabuddin did in the row in front. I gathered from his bemusement that I had made one mistake. I excused myself saying I had only followed his example. I needn't imitate his mistakes, he said with a small smile, and explained the complicated reason for his omission and my confusion.

'Do you have any further questions about your prayer?' he asked me eventually.

'No, no, the rest of it is clear,' I answered quickly.

'Nothing is ever clear as that in prayer,' my teacher said.

More Prayers

⚜⚜⚜⚜⚜⚜⚜⚜⚜⚜⚜

L ess and less often was I taken unawares by *azaan*.
My inner prayer clock was set. As I wondered where
to set myself down, geometry dispersed the throng. The
flood of people petered out on the sloping piazza in front
of the Grand Mosque. Rugs and mats were spread out,
positions taken, and rows formed, as orderly as seedlings
in a greenhouse. Everyone kept an equal distance from the
person in front of them and from the sides. Once a man
squeezed in between two pilgrims who were already rather
tightly packed, and one of them pointed to a space in the
row in front. But the newcomer stubbornly indicated the
bare concrete there until the owner of the prayer rug finally
yielded and went over to the space himself. He prayed on
the road's surface while the interloper used his clean, soft
mat.

While the preparation for prayer is an impressive
example of self-organisation, the prayer itself is an act of
considerable social symbolism. Everyone bows down to
God directly behind the soles of a fellow human, regardless
of who is higher-born or better situated. The equality of all
people is emphasised in common prayer. When a principle
is so central to a ritual, when it is performed with no degree

of compromise, how can it then be so totally ignored outside of prayer? Social abuses are a disgrace anywhere, but in Islamic countries they defile the holy order, deride the prayer and, alongside worldly failings, are an expression of religious transgression.

When everyone is in rows, feet in a straight line, the excited cacophony stops for a still intermezzo before the solo of the imam directs it into another orbit. The prayer, a structure of even and odd numbers – *And by the even ones, and by the odd* (89:3), by the living organism then, and by God: the created symmetry is rendered complete. In no other religion is prayer given such a structured framework, for the individual and for the community.

On the Hajj everyone prays together. The Haram al-Sharif is the only mosque in the world where there is no division of the sexes. In the crush all are equal, women and men. Elsewhere they pray separately, in different rooms, and if there is an opportunity to pray together, in their own home perhaps, women stand behind the men as a rule, to be shielded from their looks.

Transformations

There were still several days until the Hajj proper, the exodus into the desert, the time of purification, sacrifice and stoning; several free days to spend as we chose during which I, like many others, absolved one tawaf a day, spent as many hours as possible in the Haram al-Sharif, and on occasion read a Saudi newspaper in English. Its reports were mostly about the Muslim world. Sometimes my neighbours were Iranian women, once an Algerian foreman, another time a Senegalese student who was studying in France, and once a local committee from Indonesia. The mosque was filled up already in the early morning, a little later every square metre was taken, mostly by groups, who would take over an area and spend the entire day there, punctuating the prayers with gulps of Zamzam water. The place felt like a refuge from the haste of the world, from one's own restlessness. The stillness was a miracle; a calm sea not rippled by tides. On a good day, a single Saudi bus driver would create more noise than the gentle murmuring and padding of bare feet in the elliptical refuge.

The meditation of the other pilgrims was infectious. I too felt the need to lose myself, but didn't know what to lose myself in. I couldn't recite the Qur'an in Arabic; I would read a *sura* or some *ayaat* in translation and begin to ponder the content and meaning until I realised that I had become distracted again from the tranquillity. I tried to pray, but my prayers dried up after I had fulfilled all my promises and thought of my nearest and dearest. Praying for the peace of the world didn't seem plausible, and to pray for myself – well, it was good to discover there wasn't so much I desired. So I prayed with my eyes, looked down from the oval, open terrace of the Haram al-Sharif to the Kaaba below: the people rotated at a steady pace, as though on the turning wheel of God. I watched this *perpetuum mobile* of devotion for hours on end; the colours of the day changed their hue, I lost myself in the sight, and day turned to dusk.

In the desert – for all the air-conditioning in Mecca, you are still very much aware of the desert – the colours of the day are suddenly swept away, it seems, and shapes change. In the swift transition from day to night, the returning shadows are reconciled with the harshness of day. It is as though a palette of colour has opened and the eye is amazed by the manifold shades of white that suddenly appear in the ihram. As the mosque gleams and the skies darken when a sliver of moon teeters over a minaret tower, the new calendar day commences with a kind of magic. A bird of prey hovers between the new, burgeoning moon and the Kaaba (birds do not fly over it, and airplanes are not permitted to). When a dove nears the house of God, Ibn Jubayr wrote in the Middle Ages, one of the first authors to give an account of the Hajj, it swerves either to the right or to the left.

On the terrace, too, people circle the Kaaba, those who haven't found space below, or those in search of a change.

For a little extra room they accept the greater distance. We step among the minarets, unrushed, caressed occasionally by the feathery touch of the wind. My gaze is directed downwards and I repeat *Allahu Akhbar* without cease – no trace of footsteps are left on the light marble, every step a transient step, only the name of God remains – unchanged, unchangeable. Other feet enter the field of vision and leave again, just as fleeting, steps whose meaning is linked to the Kaaba alone, proof of what is beyond oblivion and futility. And the prayer beads slip through the fingers, over and over, knowing no end.

The Occident in the Orient

⁓⁓⁓⁓⁓⁓⁓⁓⁓⁓

The Grand Mosque is surrounded by palaces, hotels and blocks of flats, plain buildings for the most part that have firmly cemented the Western style in Mecca; both in their aesthetic appearance and their practicality, they are inferior to the old Saudi houses. Once upon a time the typically high buildings were constructed in such a way that they trapped the breeze in the upper floors, and the open, jutting-out Venetian windows filtered out the sun and allowed the air to circulate through the rooms. But air-conditioning put an end to this tradition. In Dubai, the only place this old-fashioned airing and cooling system can still be admired is at the museum where it is celebrated as an example of local innovation. Some of the buildings – in particular the Hilton Hotel across from the Abdul-Aziz Gate – borrowing from townhouses long since torn down, show a certain architectural creativity. Narrow balconies with wooden shutters, extending past the facade, were once constructed to afford the female inhabitants a cool view while retaining their discretion. Two wings of a building rise higher and higher, connected by a shopping centre several storeys high, where the wealthier pilgrims retire to imbibe the worldwide taste of Burger King, Dunkin' Donuts and Pizza Hut.

Designed like an American shopping mall, this centre offers everything a pilgrim could possibly need (food, drink, CDs of the complete Qur'an), and many more items he might crave in his life outside of the pilgrimage. At one of the side entrances, fully automated massage chairs offer five-minute respites from the rigours of prayer. There is no lack of modernity in the packed halls; McDonalds, Kentucky Fried Chicken and Wimpy are as established in Mecca as Gucci and Cardin, Longines and Swatch. The bag that encloses my prayer mat is called a New Yorker, its emblem a silhouette of skyscrapers. Every item in every shop is imported – matches, fruit juices, even the prayer mats are from Belgium. The displays, counters and cash desks are laid out just as they would be in Paris or Milan, and the surly service could be straight from a boutique in Berlin's Friedrichstraße.

It is the sheer number of pilgrims that lends the sterile shopping mall a bazaar-like atmosphere. They transform the carefully decorated, air-conditioned arcades into picnic spots; they spread their rugs in the corridors and eat their pizza, chicken or falafel in front of glass facades boasting credit-card signs. The boutiques behind them offer the finest fabrics and the most elegant of shoes; the Hajjis are set apart by their modest ihram and simple sandals, but add to the attraction nonetheless thanks to their curiosity. The ihram conceals the usual clues in appearance that divide the well-to-do from the window-shoppers – an unhappy state of affairs for some, who deal with it by sporting heavy gold watches. Some people claim that even the staunchest of Muslim believers like to ogle Western goods, hoping to expose their contempt for the Western world as hypocrisy or schizophrenia. When it comes to consumption, certainly all prejudices and antagonisms are laid aside (if Coca-Cola has a bad reputation, Pepsi steps in); asceticism is only practised on certain occasions. Yet while the superiority of Western wares may be widely accepted, this certainly doesn't equate to an acceptance of a Western lifestyle and living by secular values.

Amir

❧❧❧❧❧❧❧❧❧❧❧❧

Amir loved ice cream; especially Mövenpick's fruity flavours, but he suspected a creature of excess to be lurking within, so he usually declined my invitation. Sometimes, though, he succumbed. We treated ourselves to two large scoops each, and sat down on the steps between the two wings of the Hilton Hotel to feast on our cones. There were pilgrims on each of the steps below us, a fountain spouted a delicate spray of water into the air beside us, and the view of the largest of all mosques was framed by palm trees. We licked our ice cream, and suddenly Amir started to narrate:

'When Allah *ta'ala* created people the angels were concerned.

"Why have you created them?" they raged. "They'll only get up to mischief and destroy earth."

"Ah, but I know something you haven't the slightest idea about", Allah *ta'ala* said. "Take a close look at Paradise and tell me who wouldn't want to enter?"

The angels nodded in mute agreement.

"Yes," they said after a while, "everyone will want to enter, that's for sure."

But then Allah *ta'ala* told them about all the *mushaqqat* (hardships) involved, all the expectations a person would have to fulfil – and then Allah *ta'ala* asked a second time whether everyone would strive to enter Paradise.

"Yes, they will," the angels said pensively and were silent for a while before shouting out: "but hardly any of them will succeed!"'

Whenever Amir gave his all to recounting these parables, his eyes shone and he smiled, transformed. He experienced a profound joy in these beautiful words of wisdom. He was at peace, balanced. He couldn't understand why his father got worked up if someone trod on his prayer mat. He wouldn't have noticed, he wasn't aware of such things. They were of no importance to him. He had prayed so much recently that even his boss, a dignified, tolerant man, a Kashmiri Pandit (a member of the Brahmin caste, traditionally accepting of Sufism), had requested that he pray for him on the Hajj.

Amir didn't confide the reasons for his religious transformation to me, but they must have been powerful for him to alter his priorities to such an extent that he joined the *Tabliqh Jamaat* and moved to the desert of Gujurat for four months. Like all activists in this grassroots organisation, he had to divest himself of all worldly duties for this period and be able to fend for himself. He gave up his job and his flat. He slept in simple rooms in a village in Kutch near the mosque where he spent the remainder of his time. He hadn't seen much of his surroundings. During his entire stay he had preached only twice. When he rose to speak for the first time to this community of fishermen, workmen and unskilled workers, he found himself at a loss for words.

'I am not here,' he said finally, 'to teach you anything. I am not here to lecture. I have come to learn from you.'

The Tabliqh Jamaat – founded in 1926 in the Old City of Delhi by a rather inconspicuous and shy, yet determined man by the name of Maulana Ilias – is the largest Islamic mass movement of our times, an astonishing, unorganised emergence of millions of people who attempt to strengthen their belief by travelling to an unknown place, often in an unknown land. They have no other obligation there than to pray and enter into an exchange with the locals. The headquarters are still in Basti Nizamuddin in Delhi, now a cavernous edifice of several storeys in which an atmosphere of transience is tangible. Smaller or larger groups of men, shouldering bundles, move in or out, lay down their possessions and remain there for several hours or days before continuing on their way. Venerable Maulanas give lectures, but beyond that there are no apparent organised structures. The Tabliqh Jamaat is as successful as it is because it has taken up the principle of the Hajj and utilised it in another context. Like the Hajj, it invites Muslims to take time out, albeit at different dates, also defining it differently – yet the results are similar: a deepening of faith.

One night, Amir continued, he had seen a *djinn*, a ghost. There had been a plastic bag nearby blown around by the draught. He wanted to dispose of it as it was disturbing his prayer. When he reached for it, he was dealt a powerful blow and fell backwards. The next day he developed a high fever. He was sick for days until an elderly *mufti* recommended a healing sura from the holy Qur'an.

'You won't believe how hard I prayed,' said Amir. 'During that time tears came to me easily because I had to reflect on my responsibilities, and my failings – why had I not met the right woman – about my blunders, about all the negative points I had collected. Islam is a simple faith; it is mostly simple, but can seem very difficult when you start to dwell on all you can do wrong, all the sins you may commit. God is strict; there is no room for slip-ups. It can be read in the Qur'an, over and over again: if you do not do this, if you do not follow that, then I will punish you.'

The azaan had not yet called us, but Amir was insistent we should get to the *maghrib* prayer ahead of time, for the time directly preceding *maghrib* is ideal for personal prayer. The angels change shifts at that time, and it is good if they can tell God about our prayers directly. So we stood up, threw our napkins into the waste bin and made our way through the other consumers on the steps. The taste of strawberries stayed in my mouth for a while as I complained of my indulgence to the angels.

Ramadan

A person ought to practise modesty and humility from time to time, once a year at least. He ought to be aware of the blessings he enjoys in life and experience longing, the suffering of others, and open his heart by barring the way to the stomach. About half a year into my preparations for the Hajj the phone rang late one night, and Burhan explained in a voice laden with gravitas that the new moon had been sighted: my fasting could begin. I went through to the kitchen and prepared my early break-fast, the last meal before the fasting of the day, so that I wouldn't lose any time in the morning. I set the alarm clock for 4.30 a.m. and slept badly – my subconscious anxious that I wouldn't wake up in time. Before it rang I turned the alarm clock off and stumbled out of bed. It was the quiet-est hour in Mumbai – the monster was catching its breath, gathering its strength. The Indian Ocean was a black void behind a fading sea of light. I tried to eat as much as I could – a difficult task at this time of day. My appetite was dwin-dling even though a day without meals stretched ahead.

After *fajr* I propped myself against the window and for the first time in many years, observed how the sunrise announced itself, how the emptiness of the ocean gave way to a blurring ink, how the heavens relinquished the uniform black at its edges; then that first brief moment of twilight came in which a black thread and a white one could be told apart. From this point on not a mouthful was to be swallowed, not even one's own saliva.

Until sunset food and sex were forbidden, which I could subject myself to, but I was concerned about not drinking all day. Since I had a badly damaged kidney, I asked Burhan if I might take a single glass of water at noon.

'In Islam,' Burhan said, 'you aren't required to do anything that could be detrimental to your health. If an Islamic doctor confirms that you have to drink some water in the day, then no-one can reproach you for it. You just have to pay *fidya* for not fasting properly.'

The compensation I was to pay consisted of feeding a young, homeless man for the duration of Ramadan.

During the fasting period our teaching was put on hold and the 'ulama devoted themselves to prayer and the recitation of the Qur'an. They enjoyed the privilege of not having to work. Working Muslims take holidays or work half-days. For those with physically demanding jobs, Ramadan is torturous.

In the late afternoon we gathered at the mosque. Mats were laid down in the inner courtyard and the food everyone had brought placed in the middle. We sat next to each other in rows and waited quietly for *iftar*, the breaking of the fast immediately after sunset. In front of us was a composition of fruits and nuts, and a lentil broth called *khichdi*. The papaya was bright orange, the watermelon a succulent red – the colours gleamed as though freshly created, and the smell rising from the mats promised a bewitchingly fresh start at the end of a long, hot day. We sat motionless, our eyes lowered, lost in thought, or not thinking at all.

That first day the fasting was easy, the novelty of the experience conquered hunger. But in the days that followed I grew increasingly tired as the afternoon wore on: I couldn't concentrate, was irritable, lacking vitality. There were periods when my mind was exceptionally lucid, and other times when the weariness could be confronted only by sleep.

The *muezzin's* call was heard and we reached for a date and a glass of water. It is obligatory to break the fast immediately, a superfluous command one would presume, but in that moment there was an urge within me to hold out a little longer for the food, to draw out the delightful anticipation of that first juicy morsel, and I am sure there are people who enter a damaging ecstasy of fasting. We reached for papaya or pieces of melon from the mat, and if they were too big we broke them in two and shared them with our neighbour. The silence continued as we ate. The men who gathered there were poor for the most part. Those who had nothing to eat themselves sat at one of the mats and joined us. Apart from the Hajj itself I have experienced nothing that fuels such a sense of community.

For about 10 minutes everyone concentrated on their eating, then got up with a certain haste because the hour of the *maghrib* prayer had struck; we piled into the ablution areas and rushed into the mosque, still dripping. I always found it particularly hard to free my thoughts from the liberating scent of the papaya – I devoted my prayer to the small miracles of creation.

During Ramadan the night prayer is considerably longer, as in the course of four weeks the Qur'an is to be recited in its entirety (*salat al-tarawih*). And since the holy book cannot be read from for reference during prayer, the *hafiz* among my 'ulama brothers were very busy. Most of them had already learned the Qur'an off by heart in their very early years, and some of them, in particular Sajjid and Khalid recited in well-practised and artistic tones. They were invited to recite the *tarawih* in the wealthy homes of the town – for the women, who generally prefer to pray at home, or in some case have to, as not all mosques have a separate room for women. For all those who, like me, don't have a strong grasp of Arabic, *tarawih* is either a meditative exercise, or at times the laborious fulfillment of a duty when time could be more fruitfully spent reading the Qur'an and dwelling upon it.

I went to bed in the evenings with a groaning stomach, and what I had feared happened at the beginning of the second week: I slept in. The day that had begun in slumber ended in hunger cramps.

✂✄✂✄

The final days of the month of fasting can, according to one tradition by the name of *Iiteqaaf*, be spent entirely in the mosque. Some of the 'ulama had moved there for the final fortnight; they had hung a curtain in one corner of the mosque that kept their bags and sleeping area out of sight. They were delighted when I went to join them for the final two days. Iiteqaaf was excellent preparation for the

Hajj; I experienced the reversal for the first time in which everyday life wasn't interrupted by prayer, rather prayer was interrupted by everyday needs. And I experienced the vigilance of extreme devotion.

The first night I was woken by singsong tones. Suleiman was sitting in the mosque's inner court and reciting in a voice louder than I was used to from the others. I sat down next to him.

'There always has to be someone reciting,' he explained between two suras. A little later there was a rustling round the corner and Suleiman shot me a nervous look.

'Do you hear that? Those are the *djinns*, but they don't dare approach as long as we are speaking the words of the holy Qur'an.' And he continued his recitation.

After just one day I already felt some distance towards those who waltzed in (as it seemed to me) for the prayer, only to disappear again afterwards, at a hectic pace. We, on the other hand, formed the first row behind the imam, and although perhaps we didn't pray more fervently, our prayer was certainly more detailed. After the communal prayer we took our time, remained seated, and addressed in silence anything that had surfaced as a worry or uncertainty. It was easy to believe we were closer to God.

To experience Ramadan – a struggle that ends in reward every day – has something heroic about it. It confirms one's own Islamic identity (which explains why so many more Muslims adhere to the fasting than to the five prayers), it breaks the cast of the everyday, the circle of eternal sameness, and it ends with *Eid al-Fitr* (the great feast), complete with gifts and a banquet that makes up for all the previous privation.

All the members of Markazul Maarif had gathered in our classroom, and at the teacher's desk stood Badrudin Qasmi – the director of the organisation which provided the framework for my teaching and learning time with the 'ulama. Badrubhai, as he was known to one and all, was a baroque figure of gargantuan faith. He lived in self-evident devotion, which smothered any doubts in its powerful embrace. Together with his brothers who sat next to him, he headed a commercial empire called Ajmal, which had made a name internationally with its high-quality, alcohol-free and very costly perfumes.

The 'ulama filed past him and he fed them with a piece of unleavened bread dunked in a meat sauce. After everyone had taken a symbolic bite, we ate our meal together, and Badrubhai talked non-stop about the Hajj, among other things, and how he would have the opportunity to perform it again this year, thanks be to Allah, and to his brothers who would look after the business in his absence.

And then Badrubhai turned to me and asked: 'Have you ever been on the Hajj?'

I answered in the negative, and then without the slightest hesitation or doubt he declared: 'You'll come this year, with us!'

Pilgrims

Whenever I felt a painful dig in my back I knew that Nigeria was behind me.

'Take it easy, man,' I said to the giant from Kano whose upper body was scarcely covered by the two-meter long ihram cloth.

'Many, many people,' he grumbled in annoyance.

'If you go slow, there will be no "go slow,"' I said, punning on the Nigerian name for a traffic jam, whereupon the giant guffawed with laughter before giving me another shove that sent me flying into an Arab lady who, from within the depths of her burqu'o, shouted '*Shwey, shwey*', another expression for the commandment relevant at this time: go with care. I was reminded of the taxi driver in Nigeria who had stepped on the gas after I begged him not to race at 140 km/h on the highway from Kaduna to Onitsha.

It was fascinating to watch the different behaviour of various pilgrims in Mecca. There was such variety that you might have supposed these people had nothing in common other than the two pieces of white cloth they wore. Even the way they wore these differentiated them from one another. The black Africans managed to look relaxed even in the ihram, thanks to their athletic build, their way of walking coupled with the fact that they used the upper cloth as a scarf sometimes, draping it around their necks with an almost dandy air. The Afghans benefited from laying aside their intimidating robes – now their regular features and bright eyes were shown to advantage. The moment they pulled on their local garments their proud bearing returned, they stood up taller, feet wide apart, two heads higher thanks to their turbans. They kissed and embraced one another in elaborate rituals – the expression of a connection that went beyond Islam. In absolute contrast to the Afghans were the Indonesians, the largest Muslim population in the world, and perhaps the friendliest, judging by their openness on the Hajj. Whether from Java or Sumatra, the Indonesians were reserved, gentle, and discreet; they were soft-spoken, and even their diminutive height seemed part of their good manners: they never blocked one's view. They acted in as exemplary a manner as the Prophet (pbuh) could have wished.

As a rule the Hajj is performed by wealthy Muslims, creating the impression in Mecca that obesity is prevalent in Islam (the Anatolians are apparently enthralled by the *kadaif* and kebab). The average age is also far from representative. Usually a pilgrim must have accomplished their most important worldly duties before embarking on the Hajj. There are also suspicions that young men's visa applications are often turned down because the Saudi authorities fear they will try to stay on as illegal workers.

<hr>

Of the many brief encounters on my Hajj, the one that made the deepest impression happened on the first Friday prayer. Standing to my right was an elderly man with a bushy moustache who was carrying a travel bag with the word 'IRAQ' on it. There was nothing about him to suggest that he had enjoyed any privileges in life. His face spoke of life's tough experiences; his hands and feet were rough. He was wearing plain trousers and the material of his shirt was far too thick for the heat. We greeted one another then turned to our prayers. He devoured every word of the two richly formulated sermons that trickled through the loudspeakers onto us like honey. When we had whispered, '*Assalaamu alaikum wa rahmatullahi wa barakaatuhu*' over our shoulders, right and left, I saw that he was weeping. We embraced, as is customary in many countries after the Friday prayer, and looked at one another. I tried to smile. He turned away, my right shoulder was damp, and the greeting of peace held no promise – a few weeks later the first bombs fell on his country.

Mecca – as it was and as it is

Mecca is a town steeped in history, and yet one with no ancient buildings. Its history is not merely ignored by the prevailing teachings – it is regarded as dangerous. In an amnesia that enjoys an official stamp, believers are to pay no heed to the developments and decisions made in the 14 centuries since the Prophet (pbuh) and the *Sahabah* lived, but to trust only the Qur'an and *ahadith*, and, as a pilgrim to visit only the Kaaba – which is an artefact that goes beyond history. The desire to see the sites of the stories of the Prophet's (pbuh) passion and revelation is regarded as destructive tourism. The Saudis have destroyed what was believed to be the birthplace of the Prophet (pbuh) and consigned the burial spot to anonymity. Even King Abdul Aziz al-Saud, founder of the kingdom, lies in an unmarked grave. In Medina, once the most visited cemetery, is a lake of slabs today, a huge, bleak area stretches out behind a high stone wall like a parade ground for all the *djinns* of this world.

Likewise, Mecca is a cultural centre which has been drained of its culture. Theatre and music are frowned upon, of course, but the public baths and the coffee houses have also gone – even in the Hilton only Nescafé is served. Even desserts have suffered because of this disregard for culture – I ate the most disgusting baklava I've ever had in my life in Mecca. In the bookshops, the great Arabian thinkers of the past, and present, are nowhere to be found: thinking is a suspicious act in and of itself. The Arabs of Hijaz, to which the wonderful *mo'allaqat* poets belonged, have to contend themselves with local editions of the holy Qur'an. For the Hajj I was on, King Fahd, custodian of the two holy mosques, had distributed one million, seven hundred and seventy thousand, one hundred and sixty-eight copies of the book in 19 languages, free of charge (I received my copy at departure in Jeddah). What is unusual about this English translation are the interpretations of the text, actually a presumption with regards to one's own understanding of the Qur'an and the resulting link to God. Moreover, the Saudi interpretation often differs considerably from the classical ones. According to all other translations I know, for example, women are asked, '*not to show their charms, unless they are on the outside, and to hold their veils over their breasts*' (24:31). In the Saudi Arabian version, on the other hand, the first half sentence specifies (*ie both eyes, to recognize the path, or the outer side of the hands...*) and later the deliberately untranslated word *dschuyubihinna* is explained between parenthesis as: *their bodies, their faces, their necks, and their breasts.* And thus the wearing of the burq'o is rendered a command of God, and that is in the framework of a theology that forbids free interpretation!

The relationship of most pilgrims to the hosts of the Hajj is correspondingly ambivalent, although critical opinions are expressed with caution:

'*And if Allah were to shower his servants with abundance, they would grow arrogant on earth,*' a disgruntled Jordanian quoted from the Qur'an, having been forced to wait for hours in a local authorities' office with me.

Pilgrims from Istanbul, Damascus and Cairo regard the Saudis as parvenus, *nouveau-riche*, and lacking in civilisation. And the Saudis do their utmost to live up to this assessment through their rude and coarse behaviour. Since time immemorial the inhabitants of Mecca have been called the neighbours of God while simultaneously displaying, in this centre of faith, a measure of human weakness, greed and arrogance that provokes all idealistic pilgrims.

Ibn Jubayr wrote: 'Of all Islamic countries none is more deserving of purification by the sword of all the dirt and the spilt blood ... in this country whose people do not share the honour of Islam and covet the goods of the pilgrims and suck their blood. If there are scholars of law in al-Andalus today who claim that one is no longer obliged to go on the Hajj, then this opinion is justified by the abject manner in which the pilgrims are treated, in utter contrast to the will of God.'

Like all other Hajj authors, Johann Ludwig Burckhardt had reason to complain when he wrote: 'On the feast days he [the host] invited me to a splendid lunch in the company of half a dozen of his friends which took place in my room – and the next day he brought me the bill for the expenses of the entire meal.' And at the *khutbah* I attended in Mumbai before my Hajj, and the one in Cape Town after it, believers were warned to be vigilant that they weren't cheated on the Hajj by the *muallim* and others.

Deplorable incidents have a long tradition in Mecca. The town had always been a centre for the slave trade – the market in question was a stone's throw away from the Kaaba. When the Ottoman governor of Hijaz sent a command to the regional governor of Mecca prohibiting the slave trade, Sheikh Jamal, at that time the head '*alim* of the town, issued the following *fatwah*: suggestions such as these have rendered the Turks infidel.

Already in pre-Islamic times there was an ingenious system for kidnappings, which as time went by wasn't done away with but rather refined. For centuries nothing filled the Hajjis with more fear than the thought of robberies at the hands of the Bedouins between Jeddah and Mecca, or Mecca and Medina. The great caravans paid protection money to the respective leaders (a considerable sum allowed for in the Ottoman budget), but nonetheless all the accounts that I have read speak of nocturnal attacks on pilgrims who were stabbed and others who disappeared. No-one will claim that the Hijaz Arabs were unaware at any point in their history of the material advantages of their position as neighbours of the House of God.

Today, too, public life often bears a mark of hypocrisy, a particularly problematic evil, for the Prophet (pbuh) felt a deep aversion to hypocrisy. The prevailing ideology of Wahhabi Islam – a puritanical doctrine, named after the revivalist preacher Mohammed Ibn Abd al-Wahhab (1703–1792) – picks and chooses from the traditions on offer. Laws, the declaring of- and adhering to-, are shaped as the occasion dictates. During the first capture of Medina by the Wahhabis 200 years ago, the treasures of the Grand

Mosque were stolen, supposedly to be shared amongst the poor, but the leader, Saud, sold parts of it to the Sharif of Mecca, retaining the lion's share for himself. Although the Prophet's (pbuh) commandments are meant to be followed at all times, certain ahadith are postulated as fundamental principles, while others are simply ignored. One hadith states, for example, that one should not build a house substantially bigger than one's neighbour's so that he does not feel humiliated, and yet the immense palace of the king in Mecca dwarves not only the neighbouring buildings but even the House of God.

Another hadith says: pay those who have worked for you before the sweat on their brow has dried. Yet Saudi Arabian employers continue to owe wages to foreign workers who come in their hundreds and thousands from the poorer regions of the Islamic World as well as from some non-Muslim countries such as the Philippines. There is also a alarming number of accusations of maltreatment. In the Philippines consulate nannies bide their time, 18 months in one case, waiting for the money owed to them for six months' work or more, afraid to leave the country in case they lose their rights to claim it. And the high life of the Saudi elite break another very well known hadith: '*Allah despises those who squander their wealth.*'

Wahhabi Islam, referred to (no explanation required) as 'fundamentalism', doesn't even correspond in its rudiments to the holistic programme of Islam. Neither the absolutist monarchy nor the totalitarian suppression of free expression can find any justification in the Qur'an. The sovereign elite keep tight control of the laws, but if it suits their interests they will also turn a blind eye. The proclaimed return to original Islam reveals itself upon closer inspection to be a manipulation of religion for the sake of retaining power and controlling the masses.

But because they keep the holy sites clean and accessible, constantly improving the infrastructure while ensuring the Hajj is less dangerous and more just, the hosts often receive a great deal of approval. When King Saud came to power in 1925, legislation on the abolition of protection money was passed for the first time in history, and there were also guarantees that the pilgrim leaders would have reduced powers, and that the Sharif would no longer hold a monopoly on the Zamzam water, which used to be a costly acquisition for the pilgrims and is now handed out free of charge. The Saudis take their role as guardians of the holy mosques and sites very seriously, and shy away from no investment that could result in a safer and more comfortable Hajj. And thus gratitude is as commonly expressed as criticism.

The 8th of Dhu al-Hijjah –
The Day of Departure

The bus driver passed the microphone to an elderly man in the front row who intoned the call to pilgrimage, a call we sleepily took up.

Here I am, O' God, at Thy Command.

It was two o'clock in the morning, and the traffic flowed past. We had waited a long time.

Be ready after dinner, we had been told. We took a bath, shaved our underarms and around our genitals. We put on our ihram again, and took a second set, two fresh pieces of cloth so that we wouldn't have to wash during the Hajj. Then we rested.

Here I am at Thy Command, Thou art without associate;
Here I am at Thy Command.

We read yet again about the tasks ahead. We wouldn't leave for Mina until after midnight, we were told. We smoked and napped a little.

Praise, blessings and dominion are Thine!

Shouts echoed in the stairway. We hastened downstairs and were ushered into the buses. Then we waited some more. The night was suspended, its sidelights on.

Thou art without associate.

Just when our expectation had begun to ebb, we were on the move again. Our *Labbeik* intensified as we passed through satellite towns, brand new cloned habitations, the same the world over: tall, monotonous blocks with strips of shops on the ground floor. The buildings looked like grafted alien elements in a rugged desert, providing only small niches for settlements. Town planners, who seldom accept such restrictions, fostered the intention to widen the valleys and push back the mountains. We drove through a tunnel, through another suburb, tunnel, suburb, until we emerged in a valley so brightly lit that the night was extinguished.

Mina, hemmed in on both sides by steep hills of granite, consists of row upon row of identical tents, all to be filled with life tonight. For several days of the year Mina is inhabited by two million pilgrims, otherwise the village is a ghost town. The tents are equipped with air-condition-ing and rugs, simple but comfortable – in earlier days the pilgrims slept on the sand or mud. I was alone to begin with in the assigned tent. After morning prayers I lay down and slept.

Later in the forenoon the door was unzipped and a voice cascaded into the tent before a strong, low-set figure entered: Badrubhai and his entourage. When he spotted me he raced over, embraced me and congratulated me on the Umrah, noted with pride that my face was glowing, it was full of *nur* (light – important words he uttered only in Arabic.) However, in immediate consensus with an old friend of his, I would have to grow a beard. I protested that the beard growth on my cheeks was too patchy for a beard and would just look unsightly; he dismissed that by telling me a hadith about a man who had only a single hair in his beard, which he grew nonetheless. One day he met a wise old man on the street who laughed when he saw it. The man felt slighted and so he cut the hair.

When he met the wise man again, some time later, the older man asked sadly: 'What have you done with your beard?'

'But you laughed at me,' the man said.

'What a misunderstanding,' the wise man lamented, 'I was laughing with happiness because I was imagining angels twirling on your single hair.'

Badrubhai laughed himself, louder than the wise man of his story and told me to sit down; he spread his entourage round the tent, shouted something to his family (the women and children were separated from us by a partition) and ordered a chicken curry. In his behaviour, sweeping and warm, he was both generous and domineering at once. He wasn't one to scrimp on words or gestures. It was reassuring that he bowed down to God on a regular basis.

He'd been here for the first time in 1977, he told me over the meal.

'Had anything changed?'

'Everything has changed. Back then it had been the Mecca of old, the old crumbling houses, there was no running water, and the pilgrimage was really tough, a test, not like today, *Alhamdulillah,* today everything is very easy. It was a different Hajj back then. In Mina too, everything has improved, *Alhamdulillah.* Today it is much safer. Some years back there was a big fire, here in the Indian part, the fire raged for hours, hundreds of people died, it was thought a tarpaulin had caught fire and the tents back then burned like straw. It was bad; afterwards the Saudis had to reconstruct everything from scratch, organise everything again, *Mashallah,* all that they did for us, how much more comfortable they have made it! I can vouch for it – almost too comfortable.'

The valley was scored with wide highways, bridges, flyovers and pedestrian zones. Apart from the immense Kaif Mosque, the modern slaughterhouse and some apartment complexes which rose up from one of the hills, every free metre was taken up by tents – uniformly white tents. All Hajjis were given the same accommodation, at least all those allotted a place in a tent. Badrubhai, the millionaire, slept on a sheet next to me, he ate what we all ate (Indian curries, cooked in enormous pots).

The grey of the asphalt matched the grey of the mountains. It was the national flags at the edge of the tented area that introduced a splash of colour to the whole. If the standard clothing and accommodation were an expression of the equality of all believers and the unity within the Ummah, the flags symbolised the concept of nation – a contradiction to the traditional idea of the Caliphate according to which

Muslims of different origins and languages are one. It was no coincidence that the Turkish flag, symbol of the radical breaking-away from the political order of the Caliphate, introduced at the beginning of the 20th century under the secular leadership of Kemal Atatürk, dominated visually.

അന്തരാ

'Brother Ilias, wait!' someone called. 'I have heard about you. I really wanted to meet you. Someone from my own continent at last!'

A bony man about my age stood in front of me and introduced himself, in English, as Arif.

'And which continent might that be?' I asked.

He looked uncertain. 'You're from Germany, aren't you?'

'Yes,' I said, 'sort of.'

'Well, then, Europe, I meant. I'm from England, born and grew up there.'

Before he had finished this sentence his accent gave him away.

'How is life in Blackpool?' I asked.

'Lots of *fitna*, brother, lots of fitna' (fitna being dissention; it describes a lack of morals which caused the Prophet (pbuh) to reproach the believers.)

'What precisely?' I asked.

'Well, you know: women in short skirts and see-through tops. It is not easy being Muslim there.'

Arif was obviously frustrated and it seemed that the concentrated and omnipresent faith on the Hajj had rather intensified his frustration. At home he spent the whole day behind the counter of the family shop; beyond work, he barricaded himself behind an idea of a righteous life that was hard to achieve in reality. It was difficult following all the commandments of Islam in Blackpool – a dose of self-discipline cannot replace the communal experience. There are Islamic scholars of law who have refused a life among a Christian majority for this reason. Ibn Jubayr wallowed in compassion, anger and grief for the fate of his brothers and sisters in the Levant who in his day had suffered under the dominance of the Crusaders.

'We must look within ourselves for where the blame for the weakness of Muslims at home lies,' Arif continued. 'We are not living properly as Muslims, brother, we are not strong enough in our convictions of faith. If we set an example we could make Islam strong again and bring it to Europe. The West has a lot, but it is lacking inner strength. But we are weak unfortunately, far too weak. When the Sahabah came to China, they did nothing more than live Islam. They were the most honest traders in the market, they sold their clean rice for the same price that others sold soiled rice. Those in competition complained to the king and Muslims were forbidden to trade at the bazaar. But then the people protested, and the prohibition was rescinded. Today there are how many Muslims in China ... 20 million? Those are the descendants, the fruit of that example.'

Arif dreamed of returning home to India (he said 'returning home' even though he'd been born in England), as soon as his children had grown up, and could stand on their own two feet. But he had no answer to my question of whether it was easier to lead a pure Islamic life in Gujurat where his family was from. Sure, there would be more like-minded people around, and the distance to the mosque would be shorter, the call of the muezzin louder, shopping less tricky, but would his longing be fulfilled by this alone?

Again the time between the prayers was a vague stop-gap only partially bridged by performing everyday chores. In the late afternoon I climbed one of the hills around Mina. Some pilgrims had pitched their tents on the slopes and anchored them in place with heavy stones. Some of them were camping in the open, it seemed. They were sitting silently by their bundles of belongings. Solitary figures stood on the flat ledges, upright and taut as watchmen. Sunset was drawing nearer. When the azaan rang out from the Kaif Mosque, the figures prepared themselves for prayer, above them wisps of fiery cloud, the final edge of a fading day. The voice of the leader of the prayers echoed through the valley but we, praying in our makeshift location of a ledge or terrace, followed our own rhythm – isolated seekers who had distanced themselves from the community.

In the central currents of Islam there is no place for hermits, for solitary figures, for a life lived with one's back to the world, neither monasteries nor monks are catered for in an Islamic context. As the valley of Mina symbolises, Islam is the attempt to build a social order in which the community upholds the word of God and leads a spiritu-ally truthful life in the midst of the throng, among an over-flow of people.

The 9th of Dhu al-Hijjah –
The Day of Attestation

'Today is the day that really matters!'

Who could resist that wake-up call?

'Spend the whole day in prayer; your prayers go directly to God. And pray for me, brother!'

Everyone and everything made for Mount Arafat. Buses and trucks gathered on bridges together like brooding clouds. It was the hottest day of the Hajj, and the biggest traffic jam of humanity was happening right there in the middle of the Arabian Desert.

The cleaning brigade, in rows and columns, was out in force to see us off. The men were from Pakistan and India, and were dressed in orange. In front of them a Saudi in a long white robe gesticulated, explaining how they were to clean the camp and divided the cleaning commando into teams, while millions penetrated deeper into the desert, to purge themselves.

We really should have set off after sunrise, after *ishraq,* but we had to wait for our bus well into the morning. I sat up on the roof with the other younger men. It took us two hours to travel the 15 kilometres – many pilgrims complete this stretch on foot. The traffic barely progressed along the ring road with its multiple lanes that ascend Mount Arafat. In front of us a jeep was crawling along, its boot open and piled high with cartons. Three men were busy distributing the contents among the pilgrims. They threw several packages up to us – we tore them open and found oranges, croissants and bottles of water. We tried to share out the oranges by aiming them at buses further away, but some of the oranges fell short of their target, landing between buses and rolling into the desert. We passed the croissants and the plastic bottles of mineral water down to the women and older men below, then shared the rest among ourselves. There's a lot that hasn't changed that much in the Hajj over the years. Ibn Battuta described back in the 14th century how his caravan was accompanied by several camels, loaded with water, food and medicine for the poorest pilgrims.

The sun was high above us like an executioner, punishing our shaved heads. On all sides of the hill a single, densely populated camp stretched out where most of the pilgrims did penance – only a minority would find space on the mountain itself. The pilgrims sat in tents, hands held in front of their faces, or stood on paths and open spaces facing Mount Arafat, spared neither the sun nor their own rigorous confession.

On this mountain, this 'volcanic negative of the heavenly garden', the parents of mankind, Adam and Hauwa (Eve), after they had been driven out of paradise, find each other again after 100 years of separation – Arafat means 'recognition'. In Islam both bear equal guilt for their greed for the forbidden fruit, and it is at this place that God forgave them both. When the social position of women, as reflected in the spirit of original Islam, is moulded to fit present-day demands, this equality in fault and in forgiveness could play a significant role.

ↄ৯ↄ৯ↄ৯

When we reached our campsite, Badrubhai invited me to join him for a chicken biryani. It was lightly seasoned, and the grains of rice slipped off the chicken legs.

'Have some more,' Badrubhai said, 'you'll be needing your strength.'

After the meal everyone was left to their confession, their own honest reckonings. There was heat even in the shade; we sat cross-legged and sweated like nervous novices. Some pilgrims whispered; others moved their lips silently. Pondering my grave faults I put together a catalogue of intentions, which I then mentally corrected, expanded upon and finally modestly cut, because I knew this wasn't the place for frivolous plans with a short lifespan. All around me people had directed their attention inward – it was absolutely quiet during this time, the contemplation of the many.

The afternoon prayers signalled a change. After 'asr everyone stood up, and an elderly man was invited to speak the prayer into a loudspeaker – his voice rose in volume and intensity until everyone was close to tears and many were sobbing – a prayer that reminded us of Adam and Hauwa, named the foibles of mankind and asked God for mercy. Tears were an important expression of remorse and deeply felt sentiment. Tears helped one enter Paradise. Adam prayed on this spot for months and wept so many tears that a pool formed where the birds came to drink.

The wailing voices – the amplified leaders of the prayers – rang out from every direction. What began as a gentle kindling grew to ardent fervour. The more fiery the late afternoon sky became, the more intense our pleading. Not one of the two million people was distant from the prayers at this hour. We used the time, every last minute before the sun went down, to plead for forgiveness, to pray for the fear of God, for an easy death, for a positive report on the Day of Judgement, and for the fulfilment of prayers for as long as we lived.

With the onset of sunset, congratulations rang out: *Hajj Mubarak ... Hajj Mabruk.* The Hajj is considered complete at the end of this day. Our sins were forgiven, we were like new-born babies, and from this moment on we could refer to ourselves as Hajjis. There was a pride and contentment, as far as could be conveyed in our state of exhaustion, as though we had been freed of some great weight.

☙☙☙☙

Scarcely had the sun disappeared when the camp of emotional penitents was transformed into a beehive. Each of us on a quest for our bus. They were loaded up, boarded, or in our case it was up the ladder to the roof. A stinking haze of fumes – the drivers of hundreds and thousands of vehicles turned their motors on so that their passengers could enjoy the air-conditioning. Hajjis spluttered as they made their way through the buses.

I found a space next to a doctor, also called Ilias, and his 10-year-old son, who soon crept under his father's ihram. We congratulated one another, beamed at one another; he took his mobile phone out of his small bag and telephoned his family in Mumbai excitedly.

The 10th of Dhu-al-Hijjah –
The Day of the Sacrifice

When the sun has dipped from view, Mohammad Nasiruddin al-Albani writes in his Hajj guide, pilgrims are to leave Arafat for Muzdalifah, a village near Mina where they are to spend the night until the first prayer, peacefully, full of composure. They should be especially courteous and not push or jostle.

We sprawled on the roof, conversed light-heartedly, and laughed a lot; we were relaxed, but there was a crazy blaring of horns around us that didn't let up for a long time. The Saudi Arabian bus drivers obviously didn't read their al-Albani. We had a good view from the roof. The mood was collectively euphoric, the wives and mothers of the men around me passed up tasty snacks, which we shared, chatting. One of the young men had married recently. It was a custom in his family, as in many others, for the new bride to perform the Hajj with her mother-in-law, and to take along one of her younger siblings along. He admitted to me that he didn't always pray all five prayers back home.

'But here,' he said, 'everything is different.'

A few hours later none of the buses around us had budged – we stretched out to sleep, our ihram providing inadequate protection against the creeping cold. I was awoken by the air-stream – a gorge, craters, and around us a motorised exodus. The highway with its 10 lanes (perhaps even 12) moved like a nightmare through the archaic landscape. Soon the air-stream dropped, and we chanted the *Labbeik* in the rush-hour traffic.

Around midnight we stopped at a junction and the bus driver told us to get out. In front of us was the tented town of Mina. Where was Muzdalifah? One of the Hajjis explained to me that Muzdalifah had merged with the great tented city. The hordes of pilgrims had turned the two villages into a single inhabited area. We slid down the slope and over the scattered, shrouded bodies of the sleeping, to the nearest wash station; afterwards we assembled on the asphalt for prayers. We would have blocked the entire lane (and the vehicles wouldn't have been permitted to interrupt our prayer), had it not been for a policeman who hurried over and directed us back to the left side. The evening and night prayers were held together for once. However, there was some confusion among the older ones in our group about the appropriate number of *iqamats* and *raq'at*.

When I checked in one of the books later I discovered we had made a mistake. No wonder. The complexity of the rites is legendary: everyone expects to make mistakes. When Mullah Ali Qari, author of the most famous guide to the Hajj, discovered that he was making an obvious mistake himself on one of his pilgrimages, another pilgrim gave him the helpful advice that if he wasn't sure of a detail, he could always turn to Mullah Ali Qari.

After the prayers the women in our group lay down on mats at the side of the road to sleep, while the men set off to gather stones for the traditional stoning; I picked up my bag, not inclined to spend the night at a highway exit on the day of the climax of the Hajj.

This is the night that the Hajj comes up against a logistical barrier: pilgrims are meant to stay in Muzdalifah, only returning to Mina after morning prayers. However, Muzdalifah is just a space between highway junctions, a fictitious demarcation, marked only by a board in a pedestrian zone. Some tents are in Muzdalifah, but others are in Mina; thus some pilgrims camp in their own tents without committing an error in their rites, while others have to curl up somewhere on the sand or asphalt and await the call to prayer there. However easy the Hajj may have become in many respects, the night between Muzdalifah and Mina is a guaranteed nuisance.

Late at night there was no room left in Muzdalifah and lots of the pilgrims solved the problem by choosing to disregard the rules. A wave of people made for Mina. I looked for the 49 small stones on the slopes I would need for the symbolic stoning of the devil, but they were hard to find. When there are two million pilgrims even stones become a rarity in the stony desert. They needed to be small enough not to cause anyone pain, but big enough to reach a target five to ten metres away. I opted for stones that might be too small rather than ones that were too big.

Eventually, I slid down the slope and joined the crowd. We pushed on silently in the cold, a convoy wading through a lagoon of sleep. Many Hajjis slipped, plenty pushed or stepped on those stretched out on either side. It was the old story – the state of purity was hard to keep up. When I paused some time for tea – the Somali with his thermos flask was surrounded by shrouded figures – I asked the time. It was already three o'clock, and not worth looking for a place to sleep.

By the time I had reached the tented city of Mina it was nearly four and I was hungry. The supermarket was open. In one corner oriental sweets were piled high. I bought a generous slice of baklava, orange juice and buttermilk, and sat down on the steps to observe the impatient scurrying through the illuminated night to the stoning ahead of time. I had a grim foreboding.

The Day of Arafat, wise men say, is the most bitter day for Satan. Maybe that's true. But Satan is back in the game the next day: boisterous behaviour must be one of his favourite sins in Mina.

☙☙☙

The feast day of *Eid al-Adha*, celebrated in the whole Islamic world, is one important day in a series of momentous days during the Hajj in which the pilgrim is obliged to sacrifice an animal and to stone a pillar – two rituals that go back to a shared original story. God commanded Ibrahim to sacrifice one of his sons – according to the Old Testament it was the younger Isaac (Ishaq), while the Qur'an upholds it was Ismail, the elder. On the way to the sacrificial site Ismail is thrice tempted by the devil not to heed his father, to resist him, and each time Ismail drives the devil away with carefully aimed stones. Later when the unconditional obedience of Ibrahim is acknowledged, he is permitted to sacrifice a ram, which was a gift from God, instead of his son. The Adha, the sacrificial aspect of the tradition, is expected of all Muslims on that day, but only the Hajjis re-enact the stoning (*jamarat*).

'When you go to the jamarat now,' Badrubhai warned me in the tent, 'you'll see what an easy time of it Satan has. People behave worse than he could ever hope. Their whole behaviour contradicts the spirit of Islam.'

At quarter past ten in the morning, the newspaper reports confirmed the rumour – 22 pilgrims were trampled to death on one of the bridges leading to the pillar of the devil. At quarter to ten I was standing near the Great Column thinking: so this is how it feels to be crushed. I no longer knew where my body ended and the masses began, and much like everyone else around me, I started to panic. I wanted to thrash wildly, but something – a shred of decency or a sudden paralysis – prevented me. I could hardly take in the people around me; I only knew that every brother and every sister was my mortal enemy and my only support.

C·9C·9C·9

I set off almost immediately after hearing Badrubhai's warning. The police had managed to channel the wave of people but the Hajjis started to push fiercely as soon as they caught sight of the pillar. The closer we got, the more the crowds pitched like a rolling ship. Cries rode on the back of other cries. Any vestige of consideration or patience evaporated. Hajjis were throwing stones from far too great a distance; they didn't strike the symbol of the devil, they landed on their own brothers and sisters. Even those holding off until they got close enough to the pillar had difficulty keeping their balance to aim their stones properly. I, like most of the Hajjis, terrified by now, threw my ammunition quickly, without thinking of the obligatory prayers, or of the deeper significance of the ritual. We were supposed to stand with the Kaaba to our left and Mina to the right, and we were meant to hold the stones between our thumb and index finger, saying a prayer before each throw. But we paid little attention to the rules, our thoughts focussed simply on getting out of this rite alive. None of us resembled Ismail, the fearless son of Ibrahim; we were an army on the run, soldiers shooting their last rounds.

Attempting not to hit anyone I had thrown too hesitantly and hadn't noticed that I was being pushed further and further to the front. All at once I found myself next to the fenced-off pillar. Stones rained down on my shoulders and my neck. I held up my prayer mat and used it as a shield, using my other hand to push myself away from the fence, to avoid being crushed. I looked around. The fence was around one metre high, and the stones rattled down a funnel and fell through an opening to the street level below – we were on a bridge.

It was certainly easier getting to the stoning than it was getting away. As soon as the Hajjis had thrown their seven stones, they pushed their way through the crowds to the outside, regardless of the consequences. They used their elbows to shove those in front with all their might. They didn't let others through who were trying to pass sideways, and they struggled to force a path. Everyone grew well-acquainted with the devil within. Perhaps it wasn't incidental after all that the stones landed on pilgrims – there was more chance of hitting the devil there than in the pillar. Stones that strike the pillar are as rare as good souls, I thought, when at last I could breathe once more at the end of the bridge and my nerves had settled somewhat.

‎❧❦❧❦

'The Saudi Project for Utilisation of Sacrificial Animals, managed by the Islamic Development Bank'. A counter, like at a lottery stand. Glossy brochures were scattered around, describing the ultra-modern slaughterhouse, the planned hygiene improvements, and the distribution of meat donations. An efficient employee explained what was on offer: one sheep or a seventh of a camel. He pointed to a display with the names of the countries that would receive meat this year. Half a million animals are slaughtered every year and the meat is donated to over 20 countries – the main beneficiaries this year, as the statistics informed us, were Bangladesh, Jordan and Lebanon. It was up to me to decide where my donation would be sent. I decided in favour of my 'Slavic brothers and sisters' in Bosnia, paid $100 and received a coupon that was as intricately inscribed as a share certificate. The second duty of the great feast, Eid al-Adha, was carried out in a flash by the opening of a wallet.

Poor pilgrims collect meat themselves, or can even forgo the sacrifice and instead fast some extra days after the Hajj.

Tradition-conscious pilgrims can sacrifice their animal themselves. They have to kill it with a single, swift horizontal slit of the throat and shout out: *In the name of Allah, Allah is Great. Oh Allah, this is from me to you, please accept it from me.*

But those who perform the sacrifice themselves or fetch the meat, are also only permitted to keep a third of it and must give the rest to those in need, or to relatives and neighbours ... *and feed the humble beggars and the ashamed poor* (22:36).

☙☙☙☙

On the edge of Mina, too far away to visit out of mere curiosity, is the mechanical slaughterhouse, as well as an old-fashioned one for those who want to use their own hands. In the course of the 20th century nothing in the Hajj has changed as drastically as the sacrifice. Richard Burton's account from 1853 may be viewed as symptomatic for the conditions then:

> The whole floor of the valley bore testimony to the filthiest slaughterhouse ... swarms of flies. The blood-drenched earth began to stink repulsively. Nothing moved in the sky apart from kites and vultures. Six thousand animals were slaughtered and cut open in this devil's basin.

Just a few years after Ibn Saud had come to power in 1925, the sanitary conditions could hardly have been better.

Harry St. John Philby, a British explorer, who had worked for decades at the court of Abdul Aziz Ibn Saud, informed his readers in 1931:

> I missed the sacrificial ceremony this morning, and my personal sacrifice was offered the next day in lieu, but I must add that during the three days in Mina I have seen nothing of the great slaughter or been aware of it in any other unpleasant way. The slaughter is sensibly performed far from the camps of the pilgrims ... I saw some sheep heads lying around where they perhaps shouldn't have been, but otherwise none of the stink or the repulsive sight of sun-roasted putrefaction. The medical authorities have done their work admirably and have been awarded with the lowest number of deaths on the Hajj since accounts were kept.

All I noticed of the slaughter were large pieces of sheep or goat piled up by the open kitchen at the entrance to our camp and later turned into excellent curries in the enormous pots in which two meals were prepared for us each day.

Harry St. John Philby was a witness to a turning point in the history of the Hajj. Back in the 19th century the holy places were still prime breeding grounds for plagues and disease. From 1831, cholera posed terrible problems for the authorities in Mecca. The pilgrims arrived tired and infected, caught it or infected others in Mecca, then dispersed around the world taking the contagion with them. In 1865, 60,000 people died of it in Egypt alone. Pilgrims carried the disease to New York and Guadeloupe, but it wasn't until 1874 that the cholera epidemic became unstoppable. The streets were a wretched scene, both sides strewn with corpses. Pilgrims trying to reach Jeddah died in the desert or fell ill at the port. They were rounded up in barracks, and food and water were denied to those who had run out of money.

Nowadays, too, pilgrims die of weakness, emaciation, heart attacks or sunstroke, but since the introduction of preventative medicine there have been no further epidemics. There are prophylactic centres everywhere. The Grand Mosque itself has a medical station, and at Jeddah airport you are met by representatives from the Hajj Epidemiological Studies Centre KAIA, and Mina and Arafat also have their own state-of-the-art hospitals.

❧❧❧❧

On foot to Mecca. I walk the six kilometres, as do thousands of others, from Mina to Mecca. After a tawaf and a fresh shave of the head, I will return later that day. Almost the entire road lies in shadow. Pedestrians overtake vehicles stuck in the traffic. Just before Mecca there is a tunnel for pedestrians cut into the rock and in front of it is a small park with lush lawns and some benches. Suddenly laziness is an option and how it differs in character from the tense impatience of the previous days. I have attained the pinnacle of being a pilgrim, and with my legs outstretched I enjoy a sense of happiness and gratitude; my thoughts are simple, it's the downhill stretch, I don't need to force myself, I have time and no obligations to fulfil.

The long tunnel looks like a backdrop: all of us, simply clad in white cloth, are on our way to the Last Judgement. Past plain walls under unflattering neon light, each of us barely dragging ourselves along, our own person, the sum of our actions. It was the vision of the subterranean path to the Last Judgement, as though it existed parallel to our own existence – and not just at the end of time. As long as we are alive we are passing through this tunnel, but it is only here, between Mina and Mecca, that we are aware of it.

The tunnel leads us to an unbearably bright light. The Hajjis squint, some of them put on sunglasses, the existence of which I am suddenly reminded of, like the resurfacing of a forgotten name. We were in the centre of Mecca, above the Haram al-Sharif, at a large square, empty save for a few stalls selling prayer beads in every shape and colour.

It seemed like an eternity since I had last seen the Grand Mosque. It was nowhere near as full as when we had left for Mina. While we had been outside Mecca, the kiswah had been changed. As we said our *tawaf al-ifadha*, the tawaf at the end of the Hajj, we circled seven times around the Kaaba in its new cloth, pure silk. In earlier days the kiswah used to be donated annually by the Caliph or the Egyptian Viceroy who had commissioned it from a family in Cairo, and it was ceremoniously transported by the Egyptian caravan. Nowadays, the border is embroidered with gold thread by hundreds of hands in months of delicate work in Mecca itself, in a workshop specially created for this purpose.

In Mina, as in Mecca, there are hardly any beggars, but the few that were there, were Indian. ('The Indians, always extreme,' Richard Burton wrote, 'are either beggars or millionaires.') Up until a few years ago beggars from India were imported especially for Ramadan so that the prescribed generosity for that month wouldn't fail for lack of recipients. The beggars were apparently professionals, organised by human traders according to rules of strict hierarchy. They had to hand over their alms to receive a wage in return of approximately 400 Riyals, the equivalent of £80.

'Do not be deceived by their ihram,' an Indian standing next to me said, and sent the beggar I was talking to packing. 'They are all liars. They claim they are from Kashmir to stir compassion, for every Muslim knows Kashmir. Yesterday one turned to me, he was obviously from India, and he was carrying a child in his arms, a baby just a few months old. The man was begging for help for his child, but the child was black, black as night. It looked more Sudanese. How is that possible? I asked him. Have you ever taken a close look at your child?'

The next day I was addressed in remarkably fluent English, and in a whisper, by a young Indian man. He was a student from Northern India who had been on the road for 40 days and had run out of money. He couldn't explain to me, however, why he had stayed on in Mecca for so long if he didn't have the means to do so, and when I reminded him that a Hajji is neither permitted to beg nor to embark on the pilgrimage without sufficient funds, all of a sudden his English expertise disappeared. His discomfort made him depart swiftly after I had translated this well-known commandment into shaky Urdu.

Earlier, in the days before telephones, consulates, Western Union, and other institutions, many pilgrims depended on alms: they had either been robbed or their money had run out.

'There are all these wretched people in a state of absolute deprivation,' the Iranian Hajji Kazemzadeh wrote in 1912, 'lying almost naked by the roadside and trying to seek a little relief in the shade of the bushes, the only vegetation in the desert. Whoever passes by gives these unfortunates, abandoned to the mercy of the sun and sand, something to eat, and occasionally a generous soul takes one on his camel to Mecca.'

The 11th of Dhu al-Hijjah – The Day of the Great Stoning

B adrubhai was praying when I entered the tent.
His head was swinging rhythmically from one side to
the other, the words were pronounced with precision and
terrific emphasis; his voice came from deep within his chest.

'Show me this prayer,' I asked him when he moved from
his seated position and stretched out on his blanket.

'I can't teach it to you, you are not advanced enough yet,'
he said, but then he explained it to me nonetheless: 'The
prayer begins in the heart. You have to cleanse your heart
of everything apart from Allah. Start with the *Laa ilaaha*
[there is no God], let your chin sink to the left, and press
it down firmly to the left side to drive away the sins which
have settled as stains in your heart, and while you do this
say *illallah* [apart from God]. You have to repeat it 200
times, followed by just *illallah* 400 times, and finally 600
Allahu Allah. But you shouldn't practice this *zikr*, it is for
the advanced. You have to start small. In the first class. You
have to speak the *Bismillah* and *Subhanallah* 100 times a
day. For a whole year. Then you can progress to the more
difficult prayers. Otherwise the zikr won't work, because
you won't perform it properly. It might even have an

adverse effect. It will take a while until you reach my level. I'm in the ninth class. The 10th is the last. I can tell you, I've already reached the semi-final.'

The zikr with Badrubhai the next morning was to be one of the highlights of my Hajj. The best time for zikr was early in the morning, he explained to me, when Allah is in the first of the seven heavens and listening to those who need help. After fajr we sat down cross-legged next to each other, prayer beads in hand. Badrubhai signalled the start of prayer, slowly to begin with, as though he were feeling his way along the path we were to take, his voice soft and his upper body scarcely moving; *Laa ilaaha* sounded almost like a question, and *illallaah* was placed carefully, before it moved forward with increasing speed. Everything increased – volume, movement, emphasis – until we were following a rhythm of trance, a chorale with a crescendo, cut free of time and unanchored to any thoughts. Our zikr had lasted almost an hour, I realised. I felt invigorated and happy. It made me think of the proclamation of the great al-Ghazali: 'Music, rhythmic and soothing, brings us light that opens the heart, reveals beauty and imperfection.' In other words: music and rhythm are divine.

Once you've started with zikr, Badrubhai warned me, you'll never stop. Not even when you're travelling. The zikr that we've been praying, is just a watered down, a shorter, version of the true zikr. Out of consideration for others, for our neighbours who might have gone back to sleep. Our Prophet Mohammad, *Sallallahu alaihi wa-sallam*, says, we should always be careful that our prayers never disturb anyone else. It is very important to reveal your feelings during zikr. If you shed a tear, a single tear, this tear can lessen the hell-fire. I can say that zikr is an remedy against hypocrisy. Later, much later, you'll learn to say the zikr in silence – with your heart alone. And the highest stage is when you carry Allah's name in your every breath as you go about your daily chores, as you are talking as I am talking to you now. Then you won't need your prayer beads anymore, Allah and breathing are one. Through zikr you'll merge with Allah. He is in you when you think of him. If you inch towards him by the width of a hand, he'll approach the length of an elbow. If you approach him the length of an elbow, he'll take a step towards you. If you walk towards him, he'll run towards you.

Whosoever eats well should think of the poor.
Whoever is dressed well should think of his own
*   funeral.*
Whoever lives in good houses should think of the grave.

Tired figures drag themselves through the heat. The strain is beginning to show; the street hawkers croak out scarcely audible vending cries. A faded weariness lies in the air. Several floors of the bathing house next to the Kaif Mosque with its hundreds of cabins were taken over by Hajjis who let the water run for a long time over their exhausted bodies. Some of them put on their local clothes afterwards, others stayed in the ihram. Now that the Hajj was over I became aware of a new symbolism linked to the two white cloths: it pointed at our own deaths. One day, each of us Hajjis would lie wrapped in this in our graves. It was the only thing we'd take on our final journey. On that day, exhausted and drained by the sun, it was a comforting thought.

In the Kaif Mosque itself, an area of more than 10,000 square metres was heaving as though it were a campsite: pilgrims were eating, dozing, chatting between their bundles and bags. In Burkhardt's time, too, many people set up camp in this mosque, and strung up intestines from the columns on which they'd hang the freshly slaughtered meat to dry. The hamburger being consumed next to me seemed harmless in comparison.

Just as the sacred penetrates the mundane for the duration of the Hajj, so too does the profane creep into the religious sphere, until the two are separated only by the call to prayer, like a momentary switch of priority. After the night-time prayer the prayer room turns into a dormitory for figures shrouded in white.

⋞⋟⋞⋟

Having scarcely made it through the first day of stoning, and having experienced considerable fear, I was not looking forward to the second. In the day of the great stoning, all three pillars are attacked and the patience of the crowds is thrice tested. Late the previous evening I had walked to the pillars and inspected the area like a course that was to be tackled the next day. The best area seemed to be beneath the bridge at ground level where the flood of pilgrims wouldn't be trapped in a bottleneck. My supposition was proven true the next day; indeed, there were fewer pilgrims making for the pillars, but their behaviour was no more moderate. The irrational longing, the unnecessary rush and the aggression that the people vented towards the pillars was at a similar pitch, intensifying through repetition. A woman next to me with a fierce look on her face fired one stone after the other, showing no consideration to those present as she dealt other pilgrims sharp blows with her right elbow. Near the second pillar a steady stream of victims were being treated by four ambulances – circulatory collapse and superficial wounds. A man came towards me with a round, bloodied bandage over his left eye.

In our frenzy, announcements rained down on us through loudspeakers in all the major pilgrimage languages as we trampled the advice underfoot. Large groups were the most dangerous because they had the brute force to push their way through, shoving weaker competitors out of their path. Whenever I saw a group, recognisable usually from the corner of my eye by the patch of colour in the crowd, I tried to maintain as much distance as possible. By the great pillar stones rattled down through the funnel above; they had already half-covered the devil. At the end of the stoning he would hardly be visible – a cosmetic change *par excellence*.

ကာကာ

Arif, like me, was disgusted by his experience at the stoning, perhaps even more so since his belief in the good of the Ummah was stronger than mine. When he was annoyed he would draw his neck in while his shoulders formed a slight hunch as if every muscle from his heart to his tongue was tense.

'You have experienced,' he shouted with the passion of a travelling preacher, 'what an easy game of it *Shaitan* [Satan] had today. It is forbidden to push, let alone to wound another Muslim. Most Hajjis do not know what they are doing. Not only are they hurting their brothers and sisters, they are damaging the spirit of Islam too, and the Kaaba. To touch the Black Stone, to kiss it – it means nothing, it's absolutely worthless, a symbolic gesture, nothing more – they are ready to heap sin upon sin on themselves. It doesn't add up – it is utter madness. Far too few know what Islam is really about.'

I showed him the booklets that some young activists in the street had pressed into my hand. The selection of themes was surprising. 'The Permissible Length of Leg Coverings' was the title of one, in which a certain Dr Saleh as-Saleh described, in over 16 pages, the infernal punishments those who wear short trousers will face. False priorities – Arif and I agreed – blind pedantry. Unyielding moralists had too loud a voice while the gentle mystics spoke in whispers that were too soft to be heard.

'Tell me,' Arif asked me unexpectedly, 'what is your favourite sura?'

'Surat *al-Manu'un*,' I said.

'A good example, excellent,' he said.

> *Ara'ayt alladhi yukadhdhibu biddin*
> *Fazaalikal ladhii yadu: ul-yatiim*
> *Wa laa yahuddu' alaa ta'aamil miskiin.*
>
> *Have you seen the one who denies his faith*

He is the one who shuns away the orphan
And doesn't care about the feeding of the poor.

'What does that tell us? Consider how many sins Allah *ta'ala* could have listed to describe those weak in faith. But of them all he has chosen egotism, cold-heartedness, and the lack of social conscience. What a clear exhortation!" he exclaimed.

We were standing in a corner of the camp indulging in the small sin of a cigarette. Certainly the current crisis in Islam is also due to a deficiency in social responsibility. Although the Qur'an, even more so than the New Testament, cites social responsibility and compassionate solidarity as an individual's duty and an essential pillar of society, in most Muslim countries there is a striking discrepancy between compassionate care and indifference. Just the evening before Badrubhai had referred to the commandment with perspicacity:

'If we want to be true, we must consider the plight and well-being of our fellow human beings. The Prophet, *Sallallahu alaihi waa-sallam* said, "you are only a Muslim when you think of your brothers and their needs every morning."'

The responsibility for the good of the whole has faded into the background, while concern about one's own well-being has come to the forefront. The concept of the Ummah has become a sentimental sofa on which one can recline comfortably. Identification doesn't even extend far enough into everyday life to prevent someone from pushing his brother or arguing his position in a queue (waiting for a telephone box in one of the many telephone centres would be the perfect ground for such Hobbesian studies).

'Islam,' Arif continued in agitation, 'is followed to the letter of the law but not according to the spirit. A person gets up before sunrise to pray, but goes back to bed afterwards although fajr should be the start of a day. A person adheres to the discipline of the five prayers, but is fairly lax with discipline otherwise. A person takes painstaking care to ensure the Qur'an is not placed under things, remaining on top, and is careful not to touch it with soiled hands – but does not read it. A person is generous towards a relative but abusive to a beggar. A person scolds his children when they curse but then pays a bribe. A person is meticulous about eating halal meat but poisons his spirit with senseless television programmes. A person is careful in prayer but careless in thought.'

This inconsistency was a thorn in Arif's side and I could understand his disillusionment. In its most beautiful moments the Hajj makes you believe that a different life and a different sort of humanity is possible. Pilgrimages are among the greatest creators of euphoria. A shiver runs through the masses, their lethargy evaporates briefly; a change of direction seems possible – which makes the realization all the more sobering when everything collapses again, slipping back into its usual place.

The 12th of Dhu al-Hijjah
– The Day of the Rain

The moon rose over the valley in trails of light. I was
lying on an outcrop of rock above Mina, the heat of
the day on my back, and my thoughts on one of Amir's
favourite stories, a parable from the Qur'an: One day
Ibrahim decided to worship a particularly bright star. Yet,
as the full moon shone out brightly, he changed his alle-
giance and worshipped the moon instead. But then the
moon disappeared and the sun rose and Ibrahim turned to
the sun. As he considered his changing loyalties, he came
up with a conclusion and solution; he would worship the
power that had created the star, the moon and the sun.

Something in the sky distracted me, clouds creeping in,
heavy and menacing as they swallowed up the stars one
by one and then the moon, too. And there shall be rain, I
thought to myself amused, the full works. I raced down the
slope to our tent.

Hours later when I woke up for the second time just
before eight, I saw my prediction come true; the sky over
the desert was overcast, throwing a dark shroud over the
tented city. Then it burst and the rain started to pelt down.
Mecca is prone to storms like this one; the square around

the Kaaba has been flooded several times. In 1629, a flood wrecked the city, 500 people lost their lives and the Kaaba was destroyed. In 1877 the flood waters reached two metres in height. In the bookshops one can buy a sepia photo taken in 1941 of boys splashing around by the Kaaba, which begs the question whether the lads also swam round it seven times. In the days of the caravans certain valleys were infamous for seasonal floods. Nasir-i-Khusrao tells of countless pilgrims who drowned in a sudden flood in a place still named *Juhfa* (washed away).

'Let's take our time,' Badrubhai said. 'Everyone will be making their way back to Mecca today and there will be a terrible crush around noon. Let's wait in the tent and set off later.'

For the first time, I was left alone with Badrubhai after our fellow tent-dwellers had departed, which gave me the chance to have a peaceful conversation with him. His reference to the 10 stages that the believer can advance had aroused my curiosity. I inquired how he had progressed from one level to the next.

'Every Ramadan,' he told me, 'I travel to Deoband and spend 10 days with my Sheikh. I use the time to learn from him. I practise and practise; for hours on end. He advises me, asks me questions, and only when he is completely satisfied am I able to move up to the next class.'

I had often heard talk of Deoband; the huge Islamic seminary in that small town in northern India where all of my 'ulama brothers had studied. They spoke about Deoband as though it were a second home, expressing the greatest respect and affection. They had even taken on the surname

of the man who had founded Deoband, all of them named
'Qasmi'.

'Studying there,' Badrubhai said, 'changed my life and my
family's too, *Alhamdulilah,* and even the life of my relatives.
I would even venture so far as to say that it has influenced
my friends as well, both the Muslims and non-Muslims.'

சுஞ்சு

It wasn't curiosity alone that led me to Deoband a few
months later with Burhan; I was hoping to recapture some
of the serenity and the contented state of mind I had experienced during the Hajj. I was in pursuit of a way back to that
peaceful and focused feeling. We took the slow train from
Delhi, several hours through the dusty plains of the Doab;
a land sandwiched between the Ganges and the Yamuna.
There was nothing at the small railway station of Deoband
that hinted at the presence of one of the largest seminar-
ies in the world. A rickshaw took us through the narrow
streets of the seething, grubby old town. Bookshops and
publishers were cheek by jowl with the shops of tailors and
ironmongers. The main thoroughfare of the bazaar ended
abruptly in front of an immense edifice made from red
and white marble. An eclectic mix of architecture inspired
by the Taj Mahal, it was the recently completed seminary
mosque, large enough to accommodate as many as 3,000
students.

The campus was an oasis of order in contrast to the
chaos of the town that surrounded it. After *maghrib* the
students sat in the open classrooms grouped around inner

courtyards and memorised the holy texts by heart in dissonant sing-song tones, their torsos swaying from side to side. The neon light in the rooms illuminated the different colours of the walls, which shone blue and green when seen from the outside.

Burhan showed me around his alma mater with evident pride. We were accompanied by some of his friends from his student days who had remained in Deoband to teach. Every once in a while students would stop to ask where I was from. Following September 11th, Mohammed Afzar, an extremely eloquent and reflective man explained, 'many foreign journalists have come to visit. They were under the impression that we were training terrorists here because the *madrasas* in Pakistan where many of the Taliban received instruction are also known as Deobandi. They have no connection whatsoever to our seminary, though.'

Meanwhile, criticism of Darul Uloom Deoband (the official name) is that the lack of modernisation in Islam's teachings creates a vacuum in which the doctrine in its pure form is distanced from external influences, which in turn results in placing limitations on free thought.

'The education we offer,' Ijaz Qasmi, another teacher and also a columnist for various Urdu newspapers, explained to me, 'is one of religious instruction. The students shouldn't be too well-acquainted with worldly matters, they shouldn't be brought up in a Westernised way, but should learn to serve their own community in a simple way. Eight years are required for this, eight years of learning the holy texts: the Qur'an and its interpretation (*tafsir*), as well as the *ahadith*.

Going up to the first floor we had a view of the largest auditorium. A teacher was reading a text excerpt in Arabic and then explaining it in Urdu, the mother tongue and lingua franca of the estimated 400 million Muslims in the Indian subcontinent.

'Each hadith is explained,' Ijaz whispered to me, 'until eventually all six ahadith collections are absorbed in such detail that the students are able to judge the genuineness of any alleged hadith without looking it up.'

Discussions were not encouraged apparently. Students had to jot their questions on a piece of paper and pass it forward to the class prefect who would then check them for repetition or nonsensical comments before handing them to the teacher.

Most of the students, as I was to discover over the subsequent days, came from poor, underprivileged backgrounds. The seminary, which had always provided teaching free of charge, as well as accommodation, food and clothing, was the only chance they had to receive an education. The secular state schools in their native villages had a shortage of classrooms, teachers and teaching materials. Even those who completed the free primary school system certificate can at the very most read, write and barely count. For the majority, the alternative to the seminary is a lifelong slog as bonded or seasonal workers. In Deoband the young men (there is a smaller seminary for women in a neighbouring small town) are empowered socially – graduates bear a distinctive dignity and exude self-confidence. However, there is an air of privation and the life practised at Deoband is a humble one. Mohammed Afzar invited us to join him for a meal one evening; he shared two rooms with a colleague. Apart from two mattresses on the floor, a cooking niche and a low bookcase, they were otherwise empty. Their trunks were placed in the middle of the floor to be used as furniture. While Mohammed prepared a chicken curry – and his colleague cut up mangoes, their ripe smell filling the room – we spoke about the origins of the seminary.

The Deoband movement had come into existence in the mid-nineteenth century as a local response to the challenges of colonialism. It promoted a codification of religious education, directly based on the example of the detested British rulers. Simultaneously, it shifted its focus back to the central social pillars of Islam – justice, rejection of hierarchies, and the importance of education. It was one of the first religious institutions to use print media for its purposes, and moreover pioneered in initiating debate with scholars of other religions. Considering the feudal, hierarchical society of the day, this was a momentous achievement. With the standardisation of theological schooling, a compulsory curriculum replaced the previously private (and often irresponsible) relationship between a teacher and his students. This social call also inspired the Indian freedom struggle and led to the founding of a number of influential Islamic organisations.

There is hardly a person more aware of the implicit expectations in the aftermath as Badrubhai; his time in Deoband was not only spent – as I found out – in meditation, but also in discussions, as he was a member of the administrative consultative board, the Shura. Recently he had repeatedly pleaded the case for opening new faculties.

After a long debate his suggestions have been put into action: today graduates can embark on further studies in journalism, computing or English. A central library with state-of-the-art technology is planned, with easy access to computers.

Orthodox teachers fear that keeping pace with technology will over time lead to a liberalisation as regards content. From Badrubhai's point of view this fear is not entirely unfounded since the Deobandis who master English are generally more open to the outside world and discourse, something I also noticed from my experience. If I asked my 'ulama brothers, for example, for their honest opinion, they would voice some criticism. They complained of corruption in the entrance exams – a serious reproach since bribery is considered a sin in Islam – and about a general drop in performance. Classes were too large and the teachers just sped through the curriculum.

'Teachers are not as dedicated as they used to be,' one of my friends exclaimed, 'they have sold their spirituality and are influenced by materialism. Many of them have only money on their minds.'

This may signify that Darul Uloom Deoband has finally caught up with the global present, much to the great chagrin of its idealistic founders, no doubt.

Yet to my own chagrin, during those days in Deoband I didn't once pray the zikr with Badrubhai. Early one morning as we were making our way from the dormitory to the campus I heard the familiar rhythmic resonance coming from one of the buildings. I crept up to the window and delighted in the sound, however no sooner had I roused myself to join in the zikr, it ebbed away as some of the men came out, Badrubhai among them. I reproached him for forgetting me and my constant desire for initiation into the zikr and he apologised profusely.

'Next time,' he said.

'Until the next zikr,' became our motto.

೧೯೯೯೯

The rain had long since stopped. Badrubhai and his group were waiting for a bus to take them back from Mina to Mecca, but it wasn't due to leave until that evening. Amir, his father and I decided to return to Mecca on foot but only after we had performed the final stoning of the three pillars. We took our luggage with us; and intuitively I put on the sunglasses I had found that morning in a side pocket. We waded through plastic refuse, the Styrofoam cups crunched under our feet and the discarded juice cartons stuck to our sandals – evidently, the cleaning brigade couldn't keep up. Those who had set up a provisional camp on the side of the road were inundated with rubbish.

We held council and decided I would wait with the luggage at the mouth of the underpass while Amir and his father performed their stoning. A few minutes later they returned frustrated – it was impossible to get anywhere near the pillars. We turned around to try the bridge, but after a few steps Amir was stopped by the police. He had to hand in his bag and collect it after the stoning, a sensible plan, but I just couldn't imagine having to go through the procedure again to perform the rite, and so in an act of egoism,

I kept my own small rucksack hidden and made it through the checkpoint unobserved. We approached the pillars arm in arm. As I was throwing my stones, merely intent on completing the task as swiftly as possible, a stone sailed into the left lens of my sunglasses. The glass was dented, but my eye unharmed.

We lost each other in our attempt to make it out of the crowds in one piece. A small group of Africans found themselves in the way of the crowds heaving away from the pillars, a force to be reckoned with. The slightly-built women didn't stand a chance; they were pushed and kicked as they tried to desperately hold onto one another, and the only man with them held his hands out protectively in a helpless gesture that was touching. Out of the corner of my eye, I saw a figure clad in black fall to the ground and my throat tightened. I do not know whether it was that woman or another, but someone was crying hysterically. It was the sort of crying you never forget.

It was at this point that I abandoned the ritual. If one doesn't question a tradition that remains the same in the face of change, then that tradition ends up losing its purpose. I shook the remaining 14 stones out of my kurta pocket as I made my way to the side and hurriedly moved off.

At the far end of the stoning, by the exit, so to speak, Sudanese traders were surrounded by Hajjis who had unintentionally sacrificed their sandals to the devil and now had to purchase a new pair. The market economy was booming in the shadow of the devil.

It was a long walk to Mecca, prolonged by the heat, and I, like everyone else, was thirsty. I spied an open truck nearby distributing juice cartons; it was like a scene from a drought crisis. A countless throng of Hajjis held up their hands as though volunteers were required, and everyone was shouting to draw attention to themselves. I positioned myself in the middle, motionless, and mute, and sought eye contact with one of the young men on the loading ramp. When he noticed me, a broad grin spread over his anxious face and he nodded over. He reached into a box, grabbed several cartons of juice and threw one of them straight at me, winking.

The 13th of Dhu al-Hijjah –
The Day of the Final Tawaf

As I was going to depart the next day for Medina, I spent this, my last day in Mecca, from early morning to the late evening in the Great Mosque. I was free of all obligations and could indulge in its beauty like an art connoisseur. Every square metre of the mosque was full of ornamental detail – calligraphy, stucco, friezes, abstract patterns – it was as if the embellished walls and ceilings accompanied the pilgrims in their recitation of the Qur'an.

The basic principal was symmetry: It stimulated the senses, celebrating creation, its strict form reflecting a greater Truth. God had, as the Qur'an intimates on several occasions, shaped the world in perfect proportion. Symmetry is more than simply an aesthetic rule; it is a quality of godly creation. By applying the rules of symmetry and proportion to life, man is, so to speak, following in God's footsteps – symmetry as virtue.

In the patterns and ornaments of Islam, in the small elements of equal size displayed to effect on cloth and marble, inscribed on the outer and inner walls and into the world beyond, there are a few basic principles: balance, repetition, alternation and similitude. None of the elements is overshadowed through perspective or positioning, none is endowed with a greater significance than the others, just as no man is superior to another. The motifs are repeated over and over, just as the prayers are. The microcosm is reflected in the macrocosm. The mystery of the beauty lies within the complex and intricate relationship between the equal parts.

In order to recognise the ornament as a whole, you have to step back to view the pattern from a distance. Creation is greater than the sum of its parts. Thus the ornament of the world represents both the divine order and one's duty towards it. In all of its forms Islamic art is a eulogy and a song of praise that is able to communicate the immeasurability of God.

But to what effect and to what aim, I pondered, as I walked round the Kaaba one last time, as slowly as I possibly could, to consciously enjoy what was soon drawing to an end. The beauty encouraged contemplation, as I was aware of on this occasion and many others previously. It encouraged meditation, sharpening the senses so that an inner perception, a higher reality, could be experienced. Ibn Ishaq, the famous early biographer of the Prophet (pbuh), writes of the way Islam penetrated the hearts of those who listened attentively to the Qur'an when read, the same way splendid poetry and recitation penetrated all barriers of prejudice and fear. Beauty is a thief that steals in to relieve us of our cautious, short-sighted and narrow-minded existence.

The recitation of the Qur'an, contemplating ornaments and reading calligraphies are not intellectual experiences whereby the purpose is to gather information or guidance, rather, they are exercises in spiritual discipline. Discipline is often overlooked as a component of Islamic aesthetics. Yet discipline nourishes constancy, which in turn yields harmony and balance – both on the level of art and in one's own existence. Discipline is diametrically opposed to the hypocrisy so forcefully condemned in the Qur'an – but it also begets tasks which can be difficult to fulfill. And if people lose sight of the ideal, they lose beauty. Like a mirror of eternal truth, the beauty of ornament reveals man's failings.

Every believer is obliged to transform the larger truth to be of personal relevance, for God sees and hears everything, as is often ascertained in the Qur'an, whereas what man can perceive through his senses is limited. Thus the revelations of the Qur'an go through two refractions, as though through a prism: Firstly, Divine Truth is transmitted through the deficient vessel of language, which is human in its limitations. Secondly, the universal message must be understood by every person with their own unique idiosyncratic individuality, and all their personal slants and shortcomings. *There is a deafness in your ears,* the Qur'an says, *and a veil lies between us and you.* Through the process of *tafsir* (symbolic interpretation), man can search for a deeper, inner Truth. Tafsir literally means taking something back to its origin or roots. The Qur'an commands Muslims through its holy text to move from the outer (*zahir*) to the mysterious inner; the *batin*. By doing so, the imagination becomes the most powerful tool; with its help the symbols of beauty can be read and translated into a meaningful experience. Thus the congregation of believers can be perceived as an ornament, the greatest and most beautiful Islamic ornament of all.

Symmetry begins in oneself, in one's own movements and dealings. At the end of the *Tawaf al-Ifadha*, the farewell tawaf, I prayed, lost in and consumed by the ornament of the *Jamaat*. But a little later, leaning against one of the pillars, I began to distance myself once more. My gaze drank in the kiswah one last time, the circling of the pilgrims, the glimmer of the lights, intent on providing my memory with food for sustenance. I felt a great reluctance to leave. The Grand Mosque was an overwhelming place with which I had developed my own personal relationship; it had become a home to me – in prayer, in thought, and above all, in the imagination.

In all my journeys never did I experience such a sense of peace as I did in Mecca.

☙❧☙❧

Everything seems divided into pairs, taking on binary forms. Either you are at prayer or not at prayer. You are moving and conscious of that movement; or you are still and conscious of that stillness. You are in ihram, away from the usual norms, resembling everyone else in appearance; or conversely you are in *ihlal*, dressed according to your place of origin and personality. The days in Mecca pass with unusual clarity. The pilgrim lives in an uncompromising manner – impossible in everyday life. He samples a taste of the perfect religious life, a simple, ordered, motivated, pure life. He should, of course, apply this new perspective to his everyday life upon return – there are some who change their lives after the Hajj. Most, however, return to their normal life and the Hajj becomes a magical memory, like a wonderful spiritual holiday infused with happiness.

Journey to Medina

Although Hamidbhai had written down the name of the pick-up point, it still wasn't easy to find the bus stop. It was the middle of the night and our vague directions added to the moroseness of our taxi driver. At night Mecca seemed like Los Angeles or Singapore, a network of highways, flyovers, junctions and crossroads; bleak, all washed in cold light. In front, Amir was trying to give directions to the taxi driver in broken Arabic. We had split from the group because, for different reasons, we didn't want to spend two more weeks in Mecca. As Hamidbhai handed me my plane ticket, he made me promise to call before leaving Medina for Jeddah. I put the ticket away in a safe place without looking at it or discussing it in any detail. That was soon to prove a mistake. The taxi driver pulled up in the right lane and pointed to a parking lot on the other side. It would take another five minutes for the taxi to cross to that side, so we got out, clutching our luggage, in which 10-litre canisters of Zamzam water had been added, and climbed over the metal railing between the lanes, our only obstacle on the path to Medina.

An hour later our bus departed. The uncomfortable seats made sleep all but impossible. We stopped at a mosque service area somewhere in the desert for the fajr prayer. Soon afterwards the landscape revealed what had been hinted at; dawn draped the jagged hills with its soft colours, it was beguiling. An hour later the spell was broken – hills of rusty red were our companions all the way to the second holy city.

In stark contrast to Mecca, Medina lies in a verdant south-facing plain, lush with date palms. At around 10 o'clock we drew up at the enormous bus station on the edge of town and were kept there for two hours, as though we were goods awaiting inspection at customs. There was no explanation, but we were well catered for with a further ration of milk, juice, biscuits and cakes.

The more restless among us paced up and down in front of the bus. The wait was unbearable for a dignified old gentleman who seemed worried and downcast – he had no time to waste and had to get to Jeddah airport that same evening. He was travelling with his unmarried daughter and his haste was provoked by a recent misfortune; he had been robbed of all his money. During the stoning of Satan someone had trodden on his damaged left foot, and in his pain he hadn't noticed that his money belt – all pilgrims wear them under their ihram – had been snipped off from behind. It was only when he had got clear of the crowds after the stoning that he realised the belt was gone. It was a sad tale, but laced with unintentional humour for the man had been deputy chief of police in the northern Nigerian town of Kaduna before his retirement.

We waited in the shade of the bus, and the frustration of the Nigerian Hajji bubbled over.

'What has our world come to,' he complained, 'when thieves are at large even in the house of God?' (despite the draconian punishments!)

Even worse though, he lamented indignantly, he had seen, with his own eyes, how an attempted robbery during the tawaf had gone wrong; the knife had sliced through the pilgrim who had bled to death on the spot. But there were bad people outside Saudi Arabia, too. The man started to talk about Nigeria, about leaders provoked by some madness into using religion for their personal ends.

Young, unemployed men were encouraged to riot, they were bribed to set fire to shops and houses, to plunder. The escalating conflict was hailed as a religious struggle, and the whole world took this at face value. The conflict was fuelled by a small elite. Religion may have no influence on the immorality of politics, but can be greatly misused in the hands of politicians.

The deeply-felt pain of this serious man affected us all: he had travelled from a country of perpetual violence and disorder to a supposed oasis, only to encounter evil in the shrine itself.

After two restless hours we were transported to Medina and stopped in front of the National Adilla Establishment, an office, I surmised, where pilgrims went to have their papers inspected.

No-one on the bus knew what the next step in the procedure was. A Tunisian, on his third Hajj, said confidently that the bus would take us to our hotels. A young Saudi Arabian swept in, took note of our arrival and left. When he next appeared the only information he conveyed was that he spoke no English. The bus driver, fed up with our constant questions, rebelled; he clambered up on the roof and started throwing down our luggage, as other officials glanced our way but offered no answers. The Nigerian was bundled into a car by a member of his country's local Hajj office and driven off. Amir and I took a taxi to our hotel. It was even more ideally situated than the one in Mecca – directly opposite the Grand Mosque! Once again the sight of the Haram al-Sharif reconciled us with human behaviour.

It is not obligatory to extend the pilgrimage to Medina, but there is one very good reason to: the *Masjid an-Nabi*, the Mosque of the Prophet (pbuh), where he himself is buried along with the first caliphs, Abu Bakr and Umar. The mosque is a flat spacious building with eight slender minarets. The delicately drawn arches, finished in pink and grey stone bear a certain resemblance to Romanesque architecture. The tomb of the Prophet (pbuh) is in the southern part, beneath the famous green dome. It is said that the Wahhabis tried to destroy this dome, deeming the Prophet (pbuh) a mortal man who should not be worshipped. But two of the workers fell from the ceiling, which was taken as a divine sign to leave the dome untouched.

Other cultural treasures were not saved by signs from heaven, however; the Qiblatayn Mosque had contained two qiblas – a monument of particular historical importance from the time when the Prophet (pbuh) had first directed prayer towards the north, in the direction of Jerusalem as the Jews did, before he shifted prayer towards Mecca in the second year of the Hijra. The Wahhabis, who treat history as their deadliest foe, built over this significant mark of the

Prophet's (pbuh) momentous change – for what should not be, cannot be.

A huge square stretched out from the mosque, vehicles from the Saudi Bin Laden Group constantly at work keeping it clean – they carefully navigated their way through the sobbing figures of the praying Hajjis. To the north an identical row of modern blocks had been built – uninspired concrete slabs whose latticed windows showed an obligatory reverence to tradition. Most of these buildings housed hotels: the Hilton, InterContinental and Sheraton. The quarter exudes the charm of Berlin's new centre designed on a drawing-board. Old Medina was visible beyond, a sprawl of grey, faceless buildings sheltered by a bare mountain. To the east the old-fashioned bazaar began, the place where most Hajjis spent their time between prayers.

Since the days of the Prophet (pbuh), the inhabitants of Medina have been regarded as generally friendly, especially compared to Meccans – a fact all Muslims know whether they have been to the two towns or not. The atmosphere in Medina was certainly more relaxed, the interaction in the bazaar warmer. The manager of our hotel, grumpy and grim, was an exception. He perched by the entrance in his dirty tunic, smoking one cigarette after another, squinting at the world that continued to impose itself on him at considerable expense, with no show of the politeness or hospitality required. His demeanour had rubbed off on the staff, a collection of Saudi Arabian moaners seemingly unmoved by the sublime view and the festive occasion. The talkative, relaxed mood of the Hajjis disappeared the instant they entered – the lobby was quickly crossed – and picked up again only in the lift.

Amir and I shared the room with a certain Methusalem who had digestive problems. That may have deprived him of sleep, but obviously not of the ability to recite loudly from the Qur'an day and night. The next day, the old man woke us up at four o'clock in the morning with a mighty sura, as though we were in danger of missing the fajr prayer at five thirty. The first morning it happened I automatically washed, and hurried, still half sleep, to a yawningly empty mosque. The clock above the entrance read a quarter past four and the cleaners stared at me in astonishment.

✂✂✂✂

The wave of people in front of the graves was so powerful that we were pushed past them like driftwood. Amir clung to the railing to utter his most important prayers, but I let myself drift. Later, we lay stretched out on the soft rug in the centre of the Grand Mosque.

'If you recite the fourth kalima four times in the bazaar,' Amir remarked unexpectedly, 'you receive 125,000 good points. Do you know why? Because people in the bazaar are most easily distracted from their faith.'

He was silent for a while before his contemplative voice enlightened me further about my prayer account book:

'Here, a prayer is worth about 1,000 everyday prayers. Our prayers in the Haram al-Sharif in Mecca are worth 100,000 times more, although it is easier to pray here than it is in everyday life. We ought to spend eight days in Medina to perform the sacred 40 prayers, but I don't have time. A lousy excuse, isn't it? A sheikh once told me the story of a man who had no time. He wanted to learn the *Salat-u-Tasbiih* – a complicated prayer in which the third kalima is spoken in four *raqa't*, and the whole thing repeated 75 times. So this man asked his uncle to teach him the prayer. When he heard that it was made up of 75 repetitions he protested:

"But I can't pray all that every day."

"Alright," the uncle conceded, "then once a week."

"What, every week?"

"Alright," the uncle placated, "if that seems too much for you, then pray just once a month."

"Every month?"

"Alright, once a year."

"Does it have to be every year?" asked the man with no time.

"Alright then," said his uncle, "pray it at least once in your lifetime."'

Since we weren't travelling as part of a group, Amir and I had to take care of the official formalities ourselves. On the evening of our arrival we went, as advised, to the offices of the National Adilla Establishment. We were asked to come back the next day. The next morning the sky was unusually streaked, some clouds looked like fingerprints, others like torn leaves, as we strolled over again. We were told it was almost lunchtime and our question could only be dealt with afterwards. In the afternoon, a young man behind the counter tried to stall us off until the night prayer had been performed but we stood firm and frustrated, also under a time constraint since Amir had to fly from Jeddah Airport that night. It was brought to our attention that a lot of work had piled up and to illustrate this; a door was opened through which we saw a considerable pile of passports and papers – but also a man dozing, his head on his arms, and a group of officials arguing.

We spent four hours in that air-conditioned office. I learnt the signs on the doors off by heart, in which pride was expressed, in both Arabic and English, for the honour of taking care of the Hajjis, pledging that the welfare and comfort of the pilgrims came first. Anytime Amir or I went up to the counter we were brusquely told to be patient. Finally, an overweight young man called us over to fish our passports out of a plastic bag. My German passport would have stood out from the Indian ones by virtue of its colour, but all the passports were in wrapped in protective Cosmic Travel holders. We had to open almost every single one before finding our own. Afterwards we were told to take a seat again. Dismissed once more, we complained bitterly to the official and our noisy indignation took us straight to a number of superiors, one of them a tall man, his face long beneath the white head-covering and his apology genuine. He checked our passports and tickets carefully and discovered that Amir's flight hadn't been confirmed; he had to make his way to the Air India office with one of the officials and return with the confirmation in writing.

In the meantime I waited, and two officials waited with me on the other side of the long counter. I got up, pointed at one of the signs, then at myself and shrugged my shoulders. This provoked some sleepy mirth. The superior with the sunken cheeks rushed back and forth. Amir returned, his mission accomplished. The shift had changed and those familiar with our case were replaced by others who still needed to be persuaded of its importance.

About an hour after sundown – after Amir had explained to me at least five times why he had to be at work the next day – the superior with the thin face handed us two pieces of paper on which our names, passport numbers and the date of our departure were written. That was all we needed; these were the papers that would allow us to leave Medina. Upon producing them our passports would be returned to us at the airport. The man told us to set off from Medina at least 24 hours before our flight, apologised again and took his leave in an elaborate manner. We barely had enough time to collect Amir's luggage from the hotel and exchange a hasty goodbye.

જી

The next day I felt lonely, washed out and depleted. After noon prayers, I read from the Qur'an for a while then fell asleep in the almost empty and remarkably chilly Grand Mosque (ice-cold water circulated underground). I was awakened to find my body bathed in light. The golden dome glided almost silently to the side, creating a quadratic atrium, and I was lying in the middle of it. The afternoon sunbeams beat down on me from a cloudless sky.

Over supper – sitting with my *shawarma* on the steps that lead from the Grand Mosque to the bazaar – I was addressed by two men whose accent was unmistakably British.

'Mate, do you know the latest football results?'

'What results?' I answered with great presence of mind.

'Oh, We though you were one of us. You know, our team had an important game yesterday.'

I explained that I came from India and didn't have a clue about football but if they wanted to discuss cricket, I was more than willing. The pair looked puzzled. They were from Bradford and very passionate about a team I had never heard of. They asked where I was really from. I repeated that I was Indian and they were so fascinated by this fact that a few minutes later – also carrying their fast food – they returned to join me and bombarded me with questions. I reported on life in Mumbai, but they shook their heads.

'You can't be Indian.'

'Why?' I asked.

'You are too pale.'

'And you are obsessed with skin colour,' I said to the older one. He laughed. He conceded to this but wanted to know more about my family's origin, nonetheless. He was reassured when I told him about my Central Asian forefathers, which was not entirely untrue.

They, like me, were ready to leave Medina, and were carrying plastic bags with the last of their shopping. Their experience of the Hajj was similar to mine: the Kaaba had been overwhelming, Mount Arafat intense, and the everyday reality sobering. They found the behaviour of many Muslims outrageous, the mobile phones, the pushing and the rudeness.

'Lack of civility,' one of them said.

'Definitely,' the other affirmed.

'Takes a lot to get used to it.'

'Not sure you can ever get used to it.'

We spoke about life in Britain; their outlook differed from Arif's. I could imagine them in a stadium, as loud as any other fan, minus the cursing and boozing. Although there was plenty they didn't like – the nudity on display, racism, alcoholism – they expressed their appreciation of the civil society there and the sense of community that still prevailed.

'It might sound paradoxical,' the older one said, 'but some of the Islamic ideals are more of a reality in Britain.'

∾∾∾∾

At Medina's colossal bus station, fearing hours of incomprehensible delay, I turned to a young official for help and he took me under his wing. While he was leading me to the right office he casually mentioned, not in an unfriendly way, that this wasn't actually his job but that he wanted to help me. He just had one small request in return, if I didn't mind.

'Certainly,' I said.

'Pray for me. Please pray for me.'

'Are you married?' I asked on a sudden impulse.

'No,' he replied, 'but I would so much like to be.'

'I'll pray that you find a good wife.'

He gave me a warm little smile and turned on his heel.

Homeward bound

At the airport in Jeddah I was hit by many a sinking feeling: a Saudi Arabian official shouted at us for daring to look through the pile of passports he had emptied onto a table. He wanted it to be done in order, one passport after the other. He opened a passport, peered at all our faces then handed it to its owner. All through this time-consuming ritual I had frightening visions that my passport might not have made it from the office in Medina to the bus station, or that it had been handed to the wrong bus driver. I saw it lying in some drawer, lost amongst the passports of 99 Uzbeks. The official stared at me then chucked a document enclosed in the green Cosmic Travel protective holder at me. I tore it open: The photo was one where I had more hair on my head and less beard on my chin, but it was definitely me. Relieved I hoisted my luggage to the next counter – the Zamzam water was to be shrink-wrapped.

My confidence plummeted when I was informed by an Air India official to make my way to the charter flights at the end of the hall. Even at a distance the partly obscured large crowd at the two check-in desks was clearly visible. Up close, people showed their true colours. Three groups tripped each other up: a throng of Afghans (men only), a tour-group of Turks (mostly men) and a jumbo jet's worth of Indians (equally made up of men and women). The Afghans were waiting by the desk on the left side, separated from the others by a metal barrier. Both the Turks and the Indians had the second counter in their sight. The Turks were flying to Cologne, that much was clear. The rest I gradually deciphered from curses and threats. They were waiting for an incredibly delayed plane that should have departed the previous day. Now the Indians, whose plane was ready, were jostling to hand in their luggage, but the Turks weren't letting them through. The Indians – never short of flexible solutions – had started to throw their luggage over the barrier until there was a towering pile of green bags by by the time I got to it. It seemed the ruin of the Orient and Occident had coincided.

What I saw next filled me with relief: Hamidbhai was sitting on the scales by the counter, elbows propped on his thighs. He was sitting there as peacefully as a Mandarin on a misplaced throne, while everyone around him was aggressive and chaotic: Airport workers, Air India ground staff, leaders of the Turkish and Indian travel groups – all yelling at one another.

I pushed my way through a wall of complaints from the Turks and greeted Hamidbhai enthusiastically who displayed no pleasure at seeing me again whatsoever. He just asked what on earth was I doing there in confusion. I held up my ticket.

'No,' he shook his head, 'that was just a formality so the authorities would let you out of Medina. I told you to call me before you left. You are not booked on this flight.'

I almost collapsed.

'So what do we do now?'

'Wait, and pray. Let's see. If it doesn't work out, you can come back to Mecca with us.'

I looked around: the furious faces of the Turks, the quiet insolence of the Indians who were slowly infiltrating the narrow area, the mountains of luggage – it didn't seem fair to suffer all this in vain.

Check-in had opened for the Afghans. They stood in a disciplined, quiet queue. Having checked in their luggage, their way back was blocked by a multitude of Zamzam containers, they clambered over the barrier and cut a path through the riled Turks. Remarkably, the Turks, who had protested every move the Indians made, accepted the hustling of the Afghans without a peep. Meanwhile the quarrel at the check-in counter escalated and two men started a fist-fight. Others mediated and the two combatants beat a temporary retreat. A voice in German said, 'this is mad, totally mad.'

I turned around and saw a man with a goatee, a convert I presumed, fighting for a lost cause in the strategic struggles between the Turks, the Afghans and the Indians.

When the question of who was to check-in next was finally resolved – our flight won the battle – the Indians had to move their baggage again. The young men formed a chain and moved their belongings from right to left, avoiding the Turks as is they were the plague, while trying to give those Afghans a wide berth who were unfortunate enough to get into their way. To no avail: the Indians banged into the barrier, the Afghans tripped over the bags and the Turks looked on, unmoved and unhelpful, totally unwilling to allow their fury to wane. I tried to move some Zamzam canisters forward, but the young men said the rest of the luggage had to be dealt with first. The bags were neither weighed nor assigned a ticket, simply slapped with a sticker and carried to the back.

In the end it all worked out smoothly, the Afghans had gone, the Indian avalanche of luggage had dwindled to the occasional rockfall and the first Turkish bags were on the second set of scales at the desk. I had been nervously observing Hamidbhai the whole time in the vain hope of gauging my chances; he had left the crowd at the counter and was sitting on the floor with his assistant distributing boarding cards. I held back until he looked at me and smiled.

'Stay in touch,' he said, 'come and see me sometime in Mumbai.'

Then he handed over my boarding card with one of his ostensibly nonchalant gestures. I could have hugged him. It was only when I was on the plane that I realised how well Hamidbhai had looked after me. How typical of him. First it had seemed like I would be left behind yet here I was, flying first class.

കൈകൈ

It would have been expecting too much of the stewardess to understand: Despite her several announcements that for security reasons praying in the gangways was not allowed, one Hajji after another stood up for the short *maghrib* prayer facing the plane's tail, since our backs were turned to Mecca. Each time she tried to remind these strange passengers of the regulations she was told it would ONLY take 'Ek Minit', a brief minute. It was permissible to pray sitting down in such situations, but we fresh-faced Hajjis weren't in the mood for comfortable compromises.

To my surprise the crew members weren't Muslim – our stewardess had a Parsee name. She asked when it would be best to serve the meal and asked with REAL interest about the Hajj. But the way she looked at us bespoke our disconcertingly exotic air. An older man sitting in front of me was asked to speak a prayer into the onboard microphone and one final time we were roused as one to an overwhelming pitch last experienced at Mount Arafat. Then the food was served, the darkness swallowed us and the Hajjis dozed off.

Since the man sitting next to me showed no inclination for conversation, I leafed through my notebook and read photocopies of texts by earlier Hajj authors. I felt a brotherhood (and sisterhood: one of the most interesting accounts was by the Begum of Bhopal) both with the Muslims who had testified as with the Christians who had reported on it.

Return

We waited for our luggage. I hadn't told anyone when I would be returning, but the other Hajjis were eagerly expected. Those who knew someone from the airport staff had their hands kissed in the baggage hall, as though they exuded holiness. Burhan scolded me the next day for not informing him of my arrival time; it was a custom that the Hajji be collected. I didn't want to be the cause of a sleepless night and I was also looking forward to a quiet journey home. Hundreds of green bags moved past, in between them larger boxes with labels indicating stereo systems or televisions. The only thing missing was the Zamzam water. I waited until four in the morning. When I noticed some Hajjis leaving without their water, I went over to ask.

The Zamzam containers hadn't travelled with us, someone from the travel agency explained. He had just telephoned Hamidbhai. They would be sent along on the next flight.

Unfortunately, they never arrived despite my numerous calls to Air India. I comforted myself with the thought that my 10 litres had accompanied another Hajji to Mauritius or Malaysia.

I shouldered my light bag and stepped out. I got into a taxi and leaned back. I was suddenly aware of the fact that I hadn't slept properly for three weeks. I was so full of impressions it would take months to digest them. Just as we were crossing the bridge by our tall block of flats, the Muezzin called out from the Red Mosque by Mumbai Central Station, gathering the faithful for the morning prayers.

'Prayer is better than sleep,' he called.

'Prayer is better than sleep.'

You have spoken truly, I answered in my thoughts, and you are right, but I need to sleep now. Afterwards life will go on, and it will be a richer life.

Echoes

〰〰〰〰〰〰〰〰〰〰

Because the Islamic calendar is purely lunar, the following year's Hajj fell two weeks earlier. Much had happened in the time between: I had moved from Mumbai to Cape Town; I remained in occasional contact with the 'ulama through email and everyday life had taken over – as is the case after any time-out – far quicker than I'd hoped. I hadn't written once to Amir, nor visited Hamidbhai. It was as though part of me didn't want to mix the experience of the Hajj with other experiences. The memory has faded into the background. Only occasionally, when someone calls me a Hajji, does the pilgrimage return to me in all its intensity for some vivid moments.

When Ramadan began again – it came with more challenging fasting conditions because of the long days on the Cape – I re-read my notes and was almost overwhelmed by how intensely I could still visualise it. I longed to be back on the Hajj, and I knew I could embark on that journey once more by writing about it: This was the most powerful motivation for this book.

Today I finish it, on the day of *Eid al-Adha*; a day in which the newspapers once again report deaths during the stoning. The Imam of the oldest mosque of South Africa has called for us to pray for the safe return of the Hajjis. A few days from now, relatives will collect their loved ones from the airport upon their homecoming. And soon preparations will begin for those embarking on next year's Hajj – a climax in their lives and their faith.

And as an old saying goes, You have not truly lived until you have been on the Hajj.

Cape Town,
11th of Dhu al-Hijjah 1424
(*1st February 2004*)

Glossary

⚜⚜⚜⚜⚜⚜⚜⚜⚜⚜⚜

Ahadith	plural of hadith
Alhamdulillah	God be praised
'Alim	scholar, particularly of Islam
'Asr	afternoon prayer; part of the ritual prayer *(salah)*
Aya (Ayaat pl.)	a verse of a sura
Azaan	to inform, to call; the call to prayer by the *muezzin*
Bhai	brother (Urdu)
Bismillah	in the name of Allah, (the opener to all suras)
Burqo'	black over-garment worn by women to cover their body, and sometimes their face as well (Burqo' is the face covering and abaya is for the body)
Djinn	an invisible being of fire, like mankind there exist the devout and the unbelievers
Dua'a	personal prayer and also general supplication

Eid al-Adha	the Feast of Sacrifice, takes place on the 10th of Dhu al-Hijjah
Eid al-Fitr	the feast of that comes directly after Ramadan, a celebration for the breaking of the fast
Fajr	prayer before sunrise; part of the ritual prayer (salah)
Fatwah	religious decree issued by a qualified person
Fidya	compensation for not adhering to certain rules
Fitna	dissention caused by disagreement over Islamic matters. The results throughout Islamic history have had grave consequences.
Hadith	sayings or discourse directly attributed to the Prophet (pbuh). They serve to guide in word, action and deed also serving as an example of the ideal Muslim life
Hafiz	a person who has learned and can recite the Qu'ran in its entirety from memory
Halal	lawful or permitted in Islam
Haram	unlawful or blasphemous
Hijra	the Prophet's (pbuh) flight from Mecca in September 622 to Yathrib (Medina); it marks the start of the Muslim calendar

Hijaz	the coastal region of the western Arabian Peninsula bordering on the Red Sea; includes both Mecca and Medina
Iftar	the breaking of the day's fast after sundown, literally 'breakfast' in Arabic
Ihram	a ban, the opposite of *ihlal*. It is the sacred state of dedication in which pilgrims wear simple, white cloth during the Hajj or the *Umrah*. Women wear a simple dress.
Iiteqaaf	staying in the mosque for a period longer than the prayers or sermons last.
'Ilm	knowledge
Imam	leader, exemplary figure; leader of prayers
Iqamat	stand up, receive; proclamation prior to prayer
'Ishaa	late evening prayer; part of the ritual prayer *(salat)*
Ishraq	to enlighten; also the name of the morning prayer after sunrise
Jamaat	the community of a mosque
Jamarat	symbolic stoning of the devil
Kalima	the creed of faith
Khutbah	sermon in a mosque
Kiswah	the black material, decorated with brocade, that covers the Kaaba

Kurta Pyjama	Indian Muslims' traditional dress. Consists of wide trousers and a long shirt
Labbeik Allahumma, *Labbeik;Labbeik,* *La Sharika Laka,* *Labbeik; Innal* *hamda Wal Nimata* *Laka Wal Mulk;* *Laa Sharika Lak*	Here I am, O' God, at Thy Command! Here I am at Thy command! Thou art without other; Here I am at Thy Command! Praise, blessings and dominion are Thine! Thou art without associate
Mabruk (Mubarak)	happy one, blessed one, blessings, congratulations
Maghrib	prayer after sunset; part of the ritual prayer *(salat)*
Mashallah	literally God's will; also an expression of one's own sense of wonder or contentment
Madrassa	Qur'anic school for the education of children and youth
Miqat	the areas bordering Mecca where the pilgrim must be in ihram
Muezzin	mosque official who calls the faithful to prayer – in days gone by from the minaret, now over a loudspeaker
Mufti	an *'alim* with scholarly knowledge of Islamic law (Shariah)
Qibla	the direction of Mecca, indicated by the *mihrab*, a vaulted niche in a mosque

Raqa't	a segment of the daily prayers, a ritual cycle
Sa'ee	the running of seven stretches between the hills of Safa and Marwah in a re-enactment of Hagar's search for water and food
Sahib (Sahabah pl.)	friend, companion; mostly used when referring to companions of the Prophet (pbuh)
Salat	the ritual prayer, comprising fajr, zohr, 'asr, maghrib and 'esha
Sallallahu alaiha wa-sallam	peace be upon him, abbreviated as (pbuh)
Sharif	noble, gentle, honourable; originally a descendent of the Prophet (pbuh); in the wider sense the ruling family in Mecca from around 1200 to 1924
Sheikh (Sheika f.)	officer, male or female, respected for his or her knowledge and wisdom
Shirk	polytheism, animism
Subhanallah	God be praised
Tabliqh Jamaat	founded in 1926 in the Old City of Delhi, it is the largest mass movement and preaching groups to the present day
Tafsir	interpretation and the scholarly exegeses of the Qur'an

Tarawih	recitation of the entire Qur'an during the evening prayers of Ramadan
Tashahhud	concluding formulation in any ritual prayer
Tawaf	the seven rounds performed around the Kaaba
'ulama	plural of *'alim*
Ummah	the community of all Muslims
Umrah	to visit Mecca; the small pilgrimage which can be performed in outside the Hajj season
Wazu	ritual washing prior to prayer
Zikr	remembrance, thoughts of God
Zohr	prayer at noon; part of the ritual prayer